All Organizations
Are Public

Barry Bozeman

All Organizations Are Public

Bridging Public and Private Organizational Theories

Jossey-Bass Publishers
San Francisco • London • 1987

ALL ORGANIZATIONS ARE PUBLIC
Bridging Public and Private Organizational Theories
by Barry Bozeman

Copyright © 1987 by: Jossey-Bass Inc., Publishers
433 California Street
San Francisco, California 94104

&

Jossey-Bass Limited
28 Banner Street
London EC1Y 8QE

Library of Congress Cataloging-in-Publication Data

Bozeman, Barry.
  All organizations are public.

  Bibliography: p. 155
  Includes index.
  1. Organizational effectiveness. 2. Organization.
3. Public administration. 4. Industry and state.
5. Business and politics. I. Title.
HD58.9.B69   1987   302.3'5   86-27699
ISBN 1-55542-036-2 (alk. paper)

Manufactured in the United States of America

The paper in this book meets the guidelines for
permanence and durability of the Committee on
Production Guidelines for Book Longevity of the
Council on Library Resources.

JACKET DESIGN BY WILLI BAUM

FIRST EDITION

Code 8712

The Jossey-Bass
Management Series

Contents

Preface   xi

The Author   xix

1. The Publicness Puzzle: How the Public Status
   of Organizations Affects Their Behavior   1

2. Comparing Public and Private Organizations:
   Organizational, Personnel, and Work Context Issues   14

3. Barriers to Developing Knowledge About the Publicness
   of Organizations   29

4. Economic Authority: Understanding the Roots
   of Privateness   47

5. Political Authority: Understanding the Roots
   of Publicness   60

6. Why All Organizations Are Public: A Multi-Dimensional
   View of Publicness   83

7. A Case Example: How the Level of Publicness
   Affects Performance in R & D Organizations   107

8. Implications for Research, Management Education,
    and Effective Management   142

    References   155

    Index   175

Preface

Some organizations are governmental, but all organizations are public." Were it necessary to distill the ensuing pages to but a single sentence, I would choose that sentence. The cardinal assumption of this book is that "publicness" is a key to understanding organization behavior and management—not just in government organizations but in virtually all organizations.

Let us first consider what publicness means. The term *public* has been used many different ways in many different contexts. One of the most common usages equates public with governmental. The above paragraph makes clear that the *public = government* usage is not the one I endorse. As used here, publicness refers to the *degree* to which the organization is affected by political authority. (For the moment, let us beg the question of the nature of political authority.) A first implication, perhaps the most important one, is that virtually any organization—government, business, not-for-profit—has significant public aspects. Many organizations are both constrained and empowered by political authority. Whatever the legal status or institutional context of an organization, publicness leaves an indelible stamp on it and affects its behavior in important ways.

The notion that all organizations are public to one degree or another (and that publicness is a matter of degree) seems clear enough to me. But traditional organization theory provides ample evidence that not everyone agrees. Generic organization theory, if it treats publicness at all, views public as synonymous with government. While making more of the public-private distinction, much of public administration theory equates public organizations with government organizations. I find this a puzzling and even disappointing approach to an organizational world in which "sector blurring" is becoming as much the rule as the exception and in which new organizational forms are emerging that are not easily classified by conventional labels of government-business.

Dissatisfaction with much of traditional organization theory has been one motivation for this book. Another stimulus has been disappointment with the applied, prescriptive side of public organization theory—public management. Public management scholars tend not to be a theoretically oriented lot. Conventional wisdom, historical analysis, and experiential knowledge pervade public management thinking and practice. I have no brief against personal knowledge or historiography. But I am taken aback by public management scholars' uncritical acceptance of Wallace Sayre's dictum that government and business administration are "alike in all unimportant respects." There are, indeed, some good arguments for the distinctiveness of public management, but there are also some sound arguments for generic approaches to many aspects of management. It is not an issue that is easily sorted out.

Overview of Contents

Having provided some clues as to my motivation for writing the book, let us consider its contents. The individual chapters differ considerably in content and objective. A brief overview provides an understanding of the contribution of the individual chapters to the central concerns of the book.

The purpose of the first chapter ("The Publicness Puzzle: How the Public Status of Organizations Affects Their Behavior") is simple: to frame the issues, to present the "publicness puzzle," and to lend support to the assertion embodied in the book's title. Chapter One suggests why scholars, managers, and students should be concerned about the publicness of organizations. The effects of publicness on organizations' behavior is illustrated with a series of episodes from the aerospace industry.

Much of the research literature comparing public and private organizations is reviewed in Chapter Two, "Comparing

Public and Private Organizations: Organizational, Personnel, and Work Context Issues." The studies reviewed in Chapter Two deal with the differences between the public and private sectors in regard to organization structures, personnel structures and systems, and the context of work—in other words, most differences other than those pertaining to market environment or political and legal authority. Most research studies have dealt with the internal environment for an understandable reason: It is easier to devise a good research design to examine, say, differences in promotion rates between public and private organizations than it is to examine more fundamental issues of publicness, such as shifts in the perceived legitimacy of the state and consequent effects on the rate of government penetration of society.

Chapter Three, "Barriers to Developing Knowledge About the Publicness of Organizations," was written for organization theorists and persons who are engaged in research on the effects of publicness. The chief mission of the chapter is to identify some of the problems involved in comparative research on public organizations and some possible strategies for mitigating those problems. A secondary objective is to provide a framework for categorizing the many approaches to understanding differences between public and private organizations.

Broader economic and political factors, the elemental bases of publicness (and privateness), receive attention in Chapters Four and Five. In Chapter Four, "Economic Authority: Understanding the Roots of Privateness," it is argued that endowments of economic authority, particularly proprietary property rights, explain much about organizations and their management. A well-developed body of theory in economics (usually referred to as property rights theory) examines differences between public and private organizations and provides plausible explanations as to why their behaviors should differ. There is no similarly coherent and well-developed theory of political authority, and thus Chapter Five, "Political Authority: Understanding the Roots of Publicness," brings together disparate ideas and presents a model of the effects of political authority on organizations.

Chapter Six, "Why All Organizations Are Public: A Multi-Dimensional View of Publicness," is in some respects the most important chapter. Here the assumptions of the book are drawn together to provide an alternative perspective on publicness. Chapter Six argues that publicness is best viewed in terms of degree of political constraint and endowment affecting the organization. A concept of publicness is developed that is appropriate for any type of organization, a concept that should be able to cope with such phenomena as sector blurring and the emergence of hybrid and multi-organization forms.

Some of the concepts developed in Chapter Six are applied in Chapter Seven, "A Case Example: How the Level of Publicness Affects Performance in R & D Organizations." Using two simple measures, one indicating privateness and the other publicness, a set of R & D organizations is classified and their performance is assessed. The results indicate that "government" and "public" are not best viewed as identical and, more to the point, publicness (as measured by resources derived from government sources) seems to say much about organization effectiveness.

The concluding chapter ("Implications for Research, Management Education, and Effective Management") begins by exploring the possibilities for using the publicness puzzle as an organizing paradigm for the study of public management and then suggests the relevance of publicness theory to the practice of "publicness management." The chapter ends with a discussion of the relevance of the publicness puzzle to public management education.

Who Should Read This Book?

I hope managers will read the book. I do have realistic expectations: The studies about the amount of time action-oriented managers devote to non-work-related reading show that authors have powerful competitors for managers' time. Still, I think this book is worth managers' time. The book will prove especially valuable for (1) business managers whose responsibilities include dealing with government constraints, seeking government resources, or trying to understand political accountability; (2) government managers who deal with business as regulators, joint venture partners, supplicants, or resource providers; (3) managers of "third-sector" nonprofit organizations; (4) managers in such hybrid organizations as government-sponsored enterprises and government-owned, contractor-managed facilities.

What will managers get out of the book? They will not get much in the way of straightforward management prescription. There is a clear need for theory-based public management prescription. But this book is more concerned with helping develop the theories upon which such prescriptions might eventually be based. Still, there are some lessons. In particular, the book has something to say about allocating resources and responsibilities among organizations and sectors. Typically, such policy decisions are wrapped in microeconomic theory and determined by temporal politics. Institutional setting and organizational issues almost always get short shrift. The findings and discussion presented here suggest that public management and organizational issues demand more attention in such allocation decisions. The reader may even find some clues as to the ways in which public management issues affect policy success.

The book's chief value for managers is not, however, "helpful hints." The ideas presented here should help managers organize their thinking about their work, their organizations, and the organizations with which they interact. Many familiar and even time-honored managerial assumptions are beginning to creak with old age. In an environment in which some business organizations receive the majority of their funds from government and quake at the prospect of entering unsheltered markets, old-style "bottom line management" has less meaning. In an environment in which some government organizations seek profits and hire marketing and advertising personnel to boost their public image, traditional public administration nostrums have less relevance. This book should help managers better understand one of the major sources of complexity in organization environments: the constantly changing mix of political and market forces shaping organizations.

I hope organization theorists and public management scholars will read this book. Organization theorists almost always preach to the converted. Some theorists feel that an organization is an organization and public context matters little. Not surprisingly, people in business schools tend to hold this view and read books confirming the generic management gospel. But some theorists feel that government organizations have so little in common with other organizations that generic organization theory is naive and of little value for public management. Not surprisingly, people in public administration, public policy, and political science programs tend to hold this view and read books confirming the public-sector uniqueness gospel. My book endorses neither view.

I hope students will read the book. It is appropriate for a number of business and public management courses and some political science courses. The main feature that will appeal to students is that the book provokes. Having used a draft of the book as one of the texts for my Maxwell School public organization theory course, I can report that the book has generated spirited discussion. Invariably, public management students exhibit some interest in the nature of publicness. It is, after all, the core question of public management education. I usually begin my public organization theory course with the question "Why aren't you in a business school?" Not only does the question elicit some delight-fully droll sarcasm ("I hate money," "I couldn't meet the dress code"), it also gets the discussion going.

I have used a draft of the book as the text for a seminar in organization theory in a business school. While business students are understandably less introspective about the nature of publicness, the book nonetheless seems to stimulate productive discussions about the role of government in business and about the purposes of organization theory.

Acknowledgments

My ideas about publicness and its role in organization theory and management have been influenced by a number of persons. Stephen Loveless, Florida International University, and Michael Crow, Iowa State University, have written dissertations applying some of the ideas developed here. Their thinking has been so central to my work that each is a coauthor of a chapter in this book. Hal Rainey, Florida State University, has commented on much of this book and has greatly influenced my thinking (and

everyone else's) about the nature of public organizations. Robert
McGowan, University of Denver, read a draft of the entire
manuscript and provided many useful suggestions. I appreciate the
guidance of Jeffrey Straussman (Syracuse University), William
Starbuck (New York University), Richard Hall (State University of
New York at Albany), Howard Aldrich (University of North
Carolina), Stuart Bretschneider (Syracuse University), Todd
Holden (Syracuse University), Ralph Shangraw, Jr. (Syracuse
University), Mark Emmert (University of Colorado), and Gary
Wamsley (Virginia Polytechnic Institute and State University), all
of whom provided comments on one or more chapters. I was
fortunate to have the assistance of a number of exceptional
Maxwell School graduate students, including Joe Dole, Marc
Nicole, and William Burke. I am grateful to Eleanor Sheridan,
who typed much of the manuscript.

Finally, I am grateful to my wife, Judith Bozeman, for her
helpful criticisms ("It all seems pretty obvious to me"), and my
children, John and Brandyn, for helping me keep my work in the
proper perspective ("Why don't you write some books that make a
lot of money?").

Syracuse, New York   Barry Bozeman
January 1987

To Judith Lisle, Brandyn Lisle,
and John Hamilton Martin Bozeman

The Author

Barry Bozeman is director of the Technology and Information Policy Program and professor of public administration, the Maxwell School of Citizenship and Public Affairs, Syracuse University. He received his B.A. degree (1968) in political science from Florida Atlantic University and his Ph.D. degree (1973) in political science from Ohio State University.

Bozeman's research has been in the fields of organization theory and public management, with a particular focus on scientific and technical institutions. His previous books include *Public Management and Policy Analysis* (1979), *Investments in Technology: Corporate Strategies and Public Policy Alternatives* (1983, with Albert Link), and *Strategic Management of Industrial R & D* (1983, with Albert Link and Michael Crow).

All Organizations
Are Public

1

The Publicness Puzzle: How the Public Status of Organizations Affects Their Behavior

Does the public status of organizations significantly affect their behavior? That, in a nutshell, is the publicness puzzle. There is surely some merit to Warwick's (1975, p. 204) contention that "it is not enough to pack a briefcase with concepts and measures developed in other settings, unload them in a public agency and expect them to encompass all of the worthwhile reality to which they are exposed." But just how much of the "worthwhile reality" of organization behavior is explicable in terms of the concepts and measures of generic organization theory? How do public organizations differ from private organizations? And what are the implications for public management?

Many feel that publicness, if important at all, is not as significant an influence on organizations and their management as are a host of other factors, such as leadership style, organization size, and level of resources. Most organization theorists are as concerned about scientific generalization as they are about managerial effectiveness, and, understandably, they want some proof that publicness makes a difference (see, for example, Meyer and Rowan, 1977; Nystrom and Starbuck, 1981). However, public management scholars and practitioners, seeking to enhance managerial effectiveness, are convinced that public organizations are distinct from private organizations (for example, Allison, 1979; Lynn, 1981; Rainey, Backoff, and Levine, 1976).

Research on public management, in its current underdeveloped state, does little to convince theoretically oriented organization analysts that publicness merits their attention. Anecdotal evidence seems to say that business and government management differ substantially (see Blumenthal, 1983; Rumsfeld, 1979; Hayes, 1972; Califano, 1981); but even in business firms, political authority is close at hand. In reflecting on his experiences in business and government, Donald Rumsfeld (1979, p. 90) observes: "When I get up in the morning as a businessman, I think a lot more about government than I do [about] competition, because government is that much involved—whether it's HEW, IRS, SFC, FIC, FDA."

The Stakes

As matters stand, few pieces of the publicness puzzle are in place. There is scant evidence to buttress strongly held beliefs. The limited progress is especially disappointing in light of the many issues hanging in the balance. Consider some examples.

There has long been an interest in transferring technologies, including managerial technologies, between sectors. Management-by-objectives, program budgeting, flex-time personnel management, zero-based budgeting, and computer-based decision support systems are a few of the managerial technologies that have been transferred from private to public sector. The interest in private-sector management approaches has intensified under the Reagan presidency (Palmer and Sawhill, 1982).

Transfer and implementation of managerial technologies typically proceed willy nilly or, at best, according to the hunches of persons involved. Until a few more pieces of the publicness puzzle are in place, guesswork will be the rule more than the exception. Under what circumstances are social and managerial technologies transferrable between private and public organizations (Roessner, 1977)? Substantial case evidence indicates that some intersector transfers are dismal failures and others are ringing successes, but our knowledge of the determinants of success and failure is limited. Publicness might well mitigate the likelihood of successful transfer of technologies, but is it more relevant for some technologies than for others?

Another example of an important problem that can be elucidated through further study of the publicness puzzle is employee motivation. Researchers have reported that public employees tend to have lower levels of job satisfaction and organizational commitment than do their private-sector counterparts (Buchanan, 1974; Rainey, 1983; Porter and Perry, 1979). What accounts for this difference? Is it largely a function of differences in recruitment or differences in career selection patterns? Or is there something about the nature of work in the public sector that produces this effect? Buchanan (1974) argues that the reduced goal clarity of public organizations explains much. But Rainey (1983) reports that there is little variance in public and private managers' perceived goal clarity. Other studies (Ponzer and Schmidt, 1982; Rhinehart and others, 1969) suggest that self-selection is a major factor; that is, persons choosing public-sector employment may differ from those choosing private-sector employment. Resolution of the publicness puzzle might help clear up some of these questions.

There are many other controversies that also can benefit from progress on the publicness puzzle: Do bureaucratic control and "red tape" have different implications for public and private organizations (Buchanan, 1975a; Bozeman and Loveless, forthcoming)? Are government organizations really "immortal" (Kaufman, 1976), or do they have life cycles considerably like those of business organizations of similar size (Nystrom and Starbuck, 1981)? It is commonly argued that evaluating the effectiveness of public organizations is more difficult because there is no "bottom line," but what of business organizations seeking multiple objectives, such as profit, growth, and stability (Cameron, 1980)? Public organizations are said to have more turbulent environments than do private organizations (Whorton and Worthley, 1981), but why should we expect differences in environmental turbulence? More to the point, in what ways are public organizations' environments different from those of private organizations (Segal, 1974; Wamsley and Zald, 1973; Whetten and Bozeman, forthcoming)?

Perhaps the most important issue that could be clarified by further resolution of the publicness puzzle is the basic question of allocation of functions and responsibilities among sectors. Recent political experience has demonstrated that institutional arrangements for the provision of goods and services are not fixed and that virtually any function is, at least potentially, amenable to "privatization" (Savas, 1982). These same dramatic changes in the locus of service provisions have rarely had as their impetus a managerial or organizational theory. Decisions are made, instead, on the basis of normative economic criteria (such as public choice theory or supply-side economics), ideological conviction, or political expediency. Rarely is the allocation of goods and services determined by evidence that a function is better managed in one sector than in another. A better understanding of the effects of publicness on organizations' behavior could introduce another important term into the complex but perhaps incomplete criteria upon which service allocation decisions are made. There is no clear reason why ideology and economic theory should have hegemony over such decisions; managerial and organizational issues may be just as important.

Assumptions About Publicness

Many of the barriers to progress in the study of public organizations are no different from those faced by generic organization researchers: Problems pertaining to sampling, measurement error, and, more generally, internal validity are at least as troublesome in the study of public organizations as they are in other domains of organization research. But three broad problems are especially troublesome in research on public organizations. A first problem lies in the conceptualization of publicness. Researchers and theorists have not always been clear as to what is meant by a "public" organization. Is it a government bureau or an organization in which the public has a major stake, or is it a matter of the economic character of the goods or services delivered?

In many ways, the problem of conceptual ambiguity is a symptom of another problem: the blurring of sectors. Government and business organizations are becoming more and more similar in respect to their functions, management approaches, and public visibility (Musolf and Seidman, 1980). Private organizations are increasingly being penetrated by government policy, and public organizations are increasingly becoming attracted to quasi-market approaches. An additional element of complexity arises from this growth of "hybrid" (partly government, partly private) organizations and "third-sector" nonprofit organizations. The conceptual ambiguity that abounds among organization theorists is understandable: The real world of organization is rapidly changing and our development of concepts has not kept pace.

Perhaps the most important problem in public organization theory is the lack of fundamental explanation as to *why* public organizations differ from private ones. Much of the research comparing public and private organizations simply reports observed differences in the behavior of public and private organizations (by one or another conceptualization of publicness) and offers no theoretical explanation of those differences. Sometimes an ad hoc and narrow-gauged interpretation is presented, but rarely anything more.

This book responds to the problems cited above by presenting a conceptual framework that (it is argued) is appropriate for today's more complex organization ecology. The response is based on two fundamental assumptions. First, it is assumed that there are two fundamental sources of authority upon which virtually all organizations are based—economic authority and political authority. The authority base of the organization can be expected (for reasons to be subsequently elaborated) to have significant and pervasive impacts on organizations' behavior. A second fundamental assumption is that political and economic authority are best viewed as dimensions and, thus, that organizations are not wholly "public" or "private" but more or less public or private. Furthermore, organizations may be more public in respect to some of their activities and more private in respect to others. In short, any organization, whether government or business or some mix of the two, can be viewed in terms of "publicness dimensions."

The Influence of Publicness

With only a little hyperbole, this book's title nicely summarizes its central argument; and Chapters Five, Six, and Seven elaborate and defend the notion that all organizations are public. At this point it would be useful to provide an illustration of the publicness of organizations and implications of publicness for organizations' behavior. But where to begin? Almost any aspect of organization behavior can be affected by political authority.

As a beginning point, it seems useful to confine the discussion to the essential processes found in all organizations. But what is an essential process? Naturally, there is room here for disagreement. One approach is to say that an essential process is one without which an organization would not exist. It is, in a sense, a diagnostic characteristic of an organization. For instance, without a cell wall, a plant is not a plant; without a pouch, a marsupial is not a marsupial. But what are the defining characteristics of organizations? What is the set of attributes and activities without which the concept *organization* begins to lose its meaning?

If we can formulate a satisfactory definition of organization, the essential processes can be inferred. Many of the best-known definitions (Katz and Kahn, 1978; Hall, 1977; Etzioni, 1977; Blau and Scott, 1962) have common elements. A review of well-known definitions and distillation of common elements yielded the following: Organizations are formally structured and social collectives established to attain goals by acquiring resources from the environment and directing those resources to activities perceived as relevant to the goals.

This derived definition provides a purposeful but not necessarily rational view of organization. The goals may or may not be formalized, and they may be in the public interest, the collective interest, and/or the interest of one or more individuals; resources may be directed toward conflicting and even mutually exclusive goals; direction of resources may or may not be efficacious. Such a view of organizations is basic enough to encompass not only Weberian-style organizations but also "organized anarchies." Most important, it encompasses business, government, nonprofit, hybrid, and virtually unclassifiable organizations. According to this definition, the essential (that is, defining, irreducible) processes in organization behavior include: (1) establishing and maintaining the organization, (2) structuring the organization, (3) acquiring and managing resources, (4) setting and seeking goals. The essential processes of all organizations are subject to influence by political authority.

Chapter Six elaborates the effects of publicness (a concept of publicness developed in Chapters Four through Six) on the essential dimensions of organization behavior and discusses some of the managerial implications of publicness. But at this point it is useful to highlight the concerns of the book by considering a set of examples. The basic theme of the book, that all organizations are public, means that the concern is with government, business, not-for-profit, hybrid, and other organizations: literally all organizations. In support of that theme, let us now consider some of the public elements of private firms. The next section considers the influence of publicness on the aerospace industry (see also Bozeman, 1984).

The Publicness of Private Firms: Illustrations from the History of the Aerospace Industry

The major firms of the aerospace industry are privately held and, by any conventional concept, are private business organizations. However, in many respects aerospace firms are public, and, importantly, they vary in their degree of publicness. If one defines publicness in terms of the influence of political authority on the behavior of organizations, the aerospace industry serves as an excellent illustration of the role of publicness in private firms.

Resource Publicness in the Aerospace Industry. Dependence on political authority for its resources is a basic characteristic of the aerospace industry. Indeed, one observer (Steckler, 1965, p. 202) describes the industry as "the virtual ward of the government," but in actuality there is much variance among firms in regard to resource publicness. It is this variance that makes the aerospace

Figure 1.1. Public Funding of Aerospace Firms.

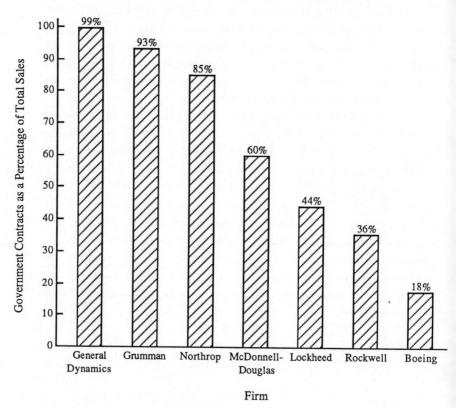

industry an especially attractive case for analysis of the effects of
publicness.

Seven aerospace firms account for more than 90 percent of
the production of American aircraft (as measured by airframe
weight). To demonstrate the differences in firms' levels of
dependence on government for their resource base, one can
examine the percentage of sales receipts derived from sales to,
respectively, commercial firms and United States government
contracts (including foreign and military sales, which are under
the control of the United States government). Figure 1.1 gives the
percentages of sales receipts for these two categories and demon-

strates the considerable variance in firms' dependence on government contracts. As demonstrated in the figure, all aerospace firms are public, but some are more public than others.

Reliance on government sales contracts represents only one aspect of the publicness of aircraft manufacturers' resource processes. Notably, firms' sales profits are subject to limitations imposed under the Vinson-Trammell Act, which provides for government financial review of the profits gained through government contracts. And the aerospace-government connection is not limited to sales. Firms are very much dependent on government for research and development funds. Several industries rely on government funds or tax credits for research and development, but the aerospace industry's degree of dependence is exceptional. Even more noteworthy is the industry's dependence on government resources for financing capital improvements. In most instances, business firms' decisions about construction of new facilities are both made and financed independently. However, in the aerospace industry, government has supported new construction and in some cases has held title to facilities leased to aerospace firms. In short, publicness pervades virtually every aspect of the aerospace industry's resource processes.

Publicness and Organization Life Cycles in the Aerospace Industry. The most familiar effect of publicness on aerospace firms is the government's role in maintaining firms that have floundered in the marketplace. The federal government's bailout of Lockheed is especially well known and widely documented (Fowlkes, 1971). Most observers agree that the federal guarantee of $250 million in bank loans prevented the bankruptcy of Lockheed—a firm that only a few years earlier had been responsible for devastating cost overruns in the production of the C-5A aircraft (Rice, 1971).

The role of publicness was just as important in the creation of the aerospace industry as it has been in the maintenance of the industry. It is common knowledge that the early aircraft industry was a child of World War I, but less well known is the extraordinary (especially for the time) steps taken by the federal government in midwifing its birth. Not only did government contracts bankroll the industry, but the federal government also provided for exceptional patenting procedures, unprecedented cross-licensing arrangements, and technical assistance. As a result, an industry that had attracted very little investor interest when subject to the normal vicissitudes of the market managed to increase investments tenfold in a single year. As late as 1914, only about 50 aircraft were produced; government-spurred production brought that figure to more than 14,000 only four years later (Simonson, 1968). During the next five decades, the growth of the industry was largely a function of a variety of government initiatives including, for example, the Air Mail Act of 1925, the Air Commerce Act of 1926, and various policies of the army air corps and the navy.

The Lockheed case and the early history of the industry underscore the same point: An understanding of organizational life cycles requires an encompassing view of publicness. In a more recent example, a major new market segment was created when, in 1980, the Federal Aviation Administration increased the allowed number of seats in commuter airlines from 19 to 58. This completely changed the economics involved in the commuter business and led to a rush to enter the commuter market. Government organizations' and business organizations' life cycles are often shaped in similar ways by external political authority.

Publicness and Structural Processes in the Aerospace Industry. The publicness of structure and structural design is well illustrated in the aerospace industry. One example is the effect of government contracting and accounting procedures on financial structures and financial management practices in aerospace firms.

Until the 1960s, "cost plus percentage profits" contracts were the norm (Bluestone, Jordan, and Sullivan, 1981). Under this arrangement, the firm's profits were based on a fixed percentage of cost. Naturally, this highly unconventional arrangement provided an incentive for contractors to keep costs as high as possible. The result was essentially a welfare program for the industry. This contracting mode was replaced with "cost plus fixed fee" contracting, a procedure that allowed the firm a predetermined fixed profit and provided no incentive (though no disincentive) for boosting costs. During Secretary of Defense Robert McNamara's tenure, the "total package procurement concept" was introduced, whereby contractors were required to incorporate costs and profits in competitive bids. For an industry accustomed to guaranteed profits, the result was massive cost overruns and, in some cases, near bankruptcy. For the aerospace industry, publicness had radically altered the traditional operation of the market.

Another example of the effects of publicness comes from facilities management. During World War II, no less than 92 percent of the aircraft industry's facilities expansion was underwritten by the federal government. In 1944, the federal government actually owned 90 percent of the facilities for the manufacture of aircraft (Cunningham, 1951). This posed an interesting problem at the end of the war—namely, how to dispose of billions of dollars' worth of surplus equipment without gutting the industry. Due to publicness, the disposal of surpluses was not simply a market problem. A contemporary account (Cleveland and Graham, 1946, p. 94) noted: "Since complete assembly lines for the production of [civilian aircraft] consist of government-owned tools and equipment, the manufacturers cannot proceed with construction until some disposition is made of these tools. On the government side of the picture, however, is the necessity for disposal to be carried out along democratic lines, i.e., all interested parties must be given an equal opportunity to participate in the sale of government equipment. The surplus disposal problem, both aircraft and facilities, thus, is a complex problem which can be solved only through the establishment and execution of a broad, over-all policy."

The postwar surplus problem illustrates some of the ramifications of the publicness of firms' structure and management practices. While the postwar example is extreme, the aerospace industry is even today highly dependent on government-owned facilities and equipment. Nor is the aerospace industry alone in its sensitivity to publicness of contracting, procurement, facilities management, accounting procedures, and personnel practices.

Publicness and Goal Processes: Shared Goals in the Aerospace Industry. Beginning in the mid-1950s, there was a sharp decline in the demand for military aircraft, and the industry was faced with a crisis shared by every major airframe manufacturer (Simonson, 1968). There were three characteristic responses: scaling down production and closing facilities, diversifying into fields far removed from airframe production, and positioning the firm to compete for now-abundant missile design and production contracts. Most of the larger firms chose the third alternative. However, the competition for missile contracts, at least initially, was quite different from that for aircraft contracts. Since the 1940s, aircraft production had been dominated by just a few firms, and experience, equipment, and vendor familiarity had by this time begun to serve as a significant barrier to the entry of new firms (Simonson, 1968). The picture was abruptly changed as firms competed for missile contracts. No one had any experience building missiles, there were no vendor "track records," and even the aircraft manufacturers' plants would have to be completely overhauled. The aircraft manufacturers could claim technical expertise, but so could electrical firms, electronics firms, and even automobile manufacturers. Indeed, even as late as 1956, less than 30 percent of missile contracts had been awarded to aircraft manufacturers (Lee, 1957). The major firms in the aircraft industry found themselves linked by a critical goal: the need to "sell" the industry's advantages for missile production in order to expand the industry's base. For a period, aircraft manufacturers closed ranks against electronics firms and other potential missile vendors, shared their technical expertise, and pursued common promotional strategies. Their success is reflected in the aircraft firms' ability to procure most of the major missile contracts during the 1960s.

In some instances, the goals of aerospace firms are affected by government regulations. Often firms resent the costs of complying with regulations, but sometimes regulations spur business. For example, as a result of new stringent emissions and noise standards handed down in 1978 by the Environmental Protection Agency, airlines were required to buy new planes or retrofit older planes with a newer generation of quieter and more fuel-efficient engines. This led to a surge in aircraft orders in 1979 (Bluestone, Jordan, and Sullivan, 1981).

Is the Aerospace Industry a Special Case? Perhaps the aerospace industry seems an easy mark. Its ties to political authority are well known and highly publicized. But if the aerospace industry is a special case, there are also other "special cases." What about universities? Many large private research universities receive a high percentage of government funds (some receive much more than the typical state university) and are subject to many of the same government policies and procedures affecting state universities. Some private universities even receive, on a formula basis, a state allocation per student. What about private hospitals and Medicare-Medicaid ties? What about the automobile industry and government loans to the Chrysler Corporation? More recently, what about the highly publicized and controversial effects of political authority on the agriculture industry? At some point, "special cases" begin to add up to generalizations.

Summary

This chapter introduced the publicness puzzle and argued that publicness, if we think of it as being derived from political authority, affects virtually every organization. To illustrate the pervasiveness of publicness, we examined the essential processes of organizations in the light of publicness. Both theoretical and managerial implications of publicness were suggested.

The basic arguments of the book now have been set out. Before advancing those arguments further in Chapters Three through Seven, the next chapter explores previous research and theory comparing public and private (usually defined as government and business) organizations.

2

Comparing Public and
Private Organizations:
Organizational, Personnel,
and Work Context Issues

Forty years ago, Paul Appleby, a successful public manager and student of public management, observed that "government administration differs from all other administrative work to
a degree not even faintly realized outside, by virtue of its public
nature, the way in which it is subject to public scrutiny and public
outcry" (Appleby, 1945, p. 7). Since that time, many public and
business executives have taken up the task of suggesting points of
distinction between public and private organizations and their
management. At the same time, a variety of avenues of research
and theory have been pursued by scholars interested in either
identifying or prescribing differences between public and private
organizations. Some alleged distinctions are broad and sweeping,
while others are narrow gauged; some claims are buttressed by
research evidence, while others are argued by force of logic,
rhetoric, or individual experience. But the list of alleged differences is by now surely a long one.

The purpose of this chapter is to review some of the many
arguments about differences (and similarities) between public and
private organizations. While the discussion is wide ranging, there
are certain emphases and conspicuous omissions. Literature that is
more prescriptive than descriptive is largely ignored in this

chapter; this eliminates from present attention everything from sophisticated public-choice theory to popular exhortations for government to be more "business-like." Another omission is studies dealing with direct effects of political and economic environments. Comparisons of public and private organizations invariably identify market incentives of private organizations and political constraints of public organizations as key differences. Political and economic authority are considered in Chapters Four and Five.

Within the self-imposed limits set above, the literature comparing public and private organizations can be set into three categories: (1) comparisons of personnel and personnel systems, (2) comparisons of tasks and work context, and (3) comparisons of organizations and their structure. The first category contains the preponderance of empirical research on public-private differences; the second category is composed largely of informal accounts and case studies; the third category is perhaps most notable for its diversity and inconclusiveness.

Comparisons of Personnel and Personnel Systems

Public organizations allegedly differ from private organizations in that public and private employees, on the whole, have different attitudes about their work and somewhat different incentive structures. It is not always clear, however, whether these differences are attributable to differences in the personnel systems—and attendant rewards and sanctions—of the respective sectors or whether the people who choose to work in the private sector are, as a whole, somewhat unlike those choosing to work in the public sector.

Workers' Attitudes. The attitudes that have been of greatest interest to researchers comparing public and private employees are those related to job satisfaction, organization commitment, and, more generally, motivation. The tone for much of this research was set by Bruce Buchanan's (1974, 1975a, 1975b) studies of business and public managers. Buchanan's studies indicate that business managers report more positive attitudes toward their organizations and identify more strongly with their organizations than do public managers.

In another study comparing work-related attitudes of public and private managers, Rainey (1979) found that government managers perceived a weaker relationship between performance and such incentives as pay, promotion, and job security. The government managers also scored lower on satisfaction with co-workers and with promotion opportunities and felt that personnel procedures in general were less flexible in regard to incentives. In a later study of 235 public and private managers, Rainey (1983) again found that public managers perceived a weaker relationship between performance and recognition and concluded that public managers' doubts that good performance will lead to higher pay and promotion account in large measure for their lower levels of job satisfaction and organization identification.

It should be emphasized that the evidence for public managers' lower levels of organizational identification and job involvement and lesser expectations about the delivery of rewards for good performance is based on just a few studies and, in some cases, draws upon samples taken from only a handful of organizations. Also, findings for state employees (Grupp and Richard, 1975) have been somewhat at odds with those for federal employees. Nevertheless, the findings are consistent enough to warrant some reflection. One plausible explanation for the relative dissatisfaction of public managers is that government personnel systems (such as the U.S. Civil Service System) are a source of frustration. Public employees are often less vulnerable than are private employees to capricious personnel decisions, but some observers feel that the same rules and procedures that protect public employees can prevent managers from punishing poor performance and rewarding good performance. Indeed, one of the chief rationales for the Civil Service Reform Act of 1978 was lessening the likelihood that the federal government would be a sinecure for the incompetent while superior employees went unrewarded (Campbell, 1978). The limited success of the act (Pearce and Perry, 1983; Ring and Perry, 1983), an initiative intended to make some government personnel policies similar to those encountered in businesses, is perhaps testimony to the inherent differences in public and private personnel management (Rosen, 1986). There is some evidence (Lovich, Shaffer, Hopkins, and Yale, 1980) that public employees, contrary to prevailing stereotypes, do not in general have negative feelings about merit-based evaluations. And public managers may be even more oriented toward achievement than are private managers (Guyot, 1962), but there is much concern about the implementation of particular subjective personnel evaluation procedures, especially procedures perceived as politicizing civil service (Lynn and Vaden, 1980; Schmidt and Abramson, 1983).

Personnel Systems, Structure, and Procedure. Another possible explanation for the lesser satisfaction of public managers is related more to the rigidity of procedures than to expectancy of reward. Not only are public managers constrained by personnel systems that limit their discretion, but they perceive that they are in general restricted more than necessary by rules and regulations. In a recent survey of more than 14,000 federal employees, a clear majority of managers and executives reported that their ability to manage is restricted by unnecessary rules and regulations (U.S. Office of Personnel Management, 1979). Interestingly, more than 70 percent of this same group agreed that they had adequate control over their work. What this may imply is that rules and regulations substitute for managerial control. Buchanan (1974) contends that hierarchical authority is severely limited in government agencies and that bureaucratic formalism is in part a response to the diminished authority. This interpretation is given some support by Rainey's (1983) findings that public managers score somewhat higher than do private managers on formalization scales.

It is a good bet that many discrepancies between public and private personnel management can be traced to differences in personnel systems. In both its contemporary structure and its origins, the U.S. Civil Service System is unlike any private personnel system. The civil service system was launched in 1889 by the Pendleton Act and was largely a response to the excesses of the spoils system that had dominated government recruitment and advancement for decades (Cayer, 1977). While favoritism, nepotism, and cliquishness occur in the private sector, nothing quite like the spoils system has ruled business personnel practices. The merit system that evolved after the creation of the civil service differs from most private personnel systems. Such practices as veterans' preference and "the rule of three" are obvious differences, but the system of grades, examinations, and safeguards on public employee rights and job security bears little resemblance to private personnel systems. Perhaps most important of all is the limited personnel authority of government's line managers and the administration of personnel functions by agencies other than the agency to which the employee is assigned. Considering such factors as the disjunction between political and career public employees, the limited ability of public employees to strike, heterogeneous public employees' unions (many including managerial personnel), and the standardized pay schedule for government employees, public personnel systems differ significantly from those of private organizations.

Self-Selection. It seems reasonable to expect that persons pursuing a career in government begin with somewhat different motivations and values from those choosing the private sector. Government policies, including personnel policies, can affect behavior, and public employees are conditioned by their work environment and by fellow employees' expectations. But the "raw material" may be somewhat different in public and private sectors. One study (Rawls, Ullrich, and Nelson, 1975) of graduate students' attitudes and values found significant differences between those intending to pursue business careers and those planning to work in government or nonprofit organizations: The public-sector-oriented students scored higher on dominance, status seeking, and flexibility, were more interested in being change agents, showed more skill in change-related activities, and were less oriented toward wealth and personal monetary gain. There is no reason to believe that government or business careers are equally attractive to everyone and, thus, one can expect certain differences related to self-selection.

Findings for precareer students are complemented by those for government employees. One well-known study (Kilpatrick,

Cummings, and Jennings, 1964), perhaps now a bit dated, found that, in comparison to the general public, federal employees are more concerned with duty and social goals and less concerned with financial reward. More recently, Rainey (1983) found that public managers attach greater importance to service and lower importance to financial rewards. Perhaps the "public service ethic" is something more than a myth.

Finally, self-selection effects seem to work not only in respect to the choice of a public service career but also in the choice to remain in the face of external change. A recent study (Lowery and Rusbult, 1986) of federal civil servants' responses to the Reagan administration indicated systematic effects on turnover and loyalty.

Comparisons of Tasks and Work Contexts

Empirical research on differences in the work contexts of public and private organizations is not common. Arguments about the scope and pace of work, visibility, and differences in time frame are not easily addressed by rigorous research designs. On the one hand, research is not required to determine that there are, for example, electoral cycles that influence public-sector organizations. But, on the other hand, exceedingly complex (and expensive) research designs would be required to determine, for example, exactly how electorally based executive succession in the public sector differs in its effects from executive succession in private organizations. In short, it is predictable that the dialogue about differences in work context hinges on anecdotes, analogies, and reports of personal experiences.

Time Frame and Pace of Work. Bruce Adams (1979, p. 546) provides a nice summary of a frequently cited difference between public- and private-sector management: "In Washington, the urgent drives out the important. The short term demands on the top policy maker are staggering. In a very real sense, our top public officials in Congress and the executive branch become the prisoners of others."

The pace of top officials is sometimes staggering, but then why should we expect that top corporate executives would be any less pressured? There are at least a couple of "pace accelerators" that are more often experienced by public than by private managers. First, the public manager is usually more subject to scrutiny from the mass media and from a wide array of interest groups that have a stake in the public manager's decisions (Blumenthal, 1983; Lau, Newman, and Broedling, 1980). This visibility (about which more will be said in a subsequent section) is one of the factors that can affect the pace of work in the public sector. When people are watching, especially millions of people, it is difficult to be reflective. The public and the media can easily interpret reflection as inaction; thus, it often seems better to do something—something visible—than to ruminate. Sometimes that something involves nothing more than appointing a study commission or a "blue ribbon" panel—surrogate thinkers; but appointing leaves historical traces, whereas thinking does not (unless thoughts are shared).

Probably the most important differences in the time frames of public- and private-sector managers are related to the political cycles of government. The appropriation process generally operates on an annual basis. Congress turns over every two years, and the presidency is subject to change every four years. There is constant pressure to achieve quick results—results that can help the agency receive a larger share in the next round of appropriations; results that may be possible only so long as congressional allies remain entrenched; results that can help reelect a president. The ballot box is not as swift as the Neilsen ratings, but it is even surer. If no one "tunes in" to a public policy during its early phases, there is a great likelihood that neither the policy nor the policy maker will have its option renewed. Sometimes elected officials and public managers try to buy time for their programs. Consider, for example, President Reagan's frequent allusion to "thirty years of Democratic mismanagement of the economy"—a clear plea to give his own program more time to take effect. Of course, such attempts are usually in vain.

More often public managers snip the already short wick of their candle by making rash claims for their programs (Califano,

1981). This is a "rational" response, at least in the short run. Legislators and executive superiors must be convinced that new programs are worthwhile and, with so many apparently worthwhile programs competing for scarce funds, it is the rare public manager who can resist the urge to make exaggerated claims for a pet program.

Pressures are also created by the organization of government. Since agencies often are organized according to policy mission and with policy specializations taking precedence over general management functions, delegation of authority is more complicated and usually more difficult. This point is well made in an essay (Kogod and Caulfield, 1982, p. 983) comparing the roles of the public and private sectors: "In the private sector, a well-run organization allows decisions to be made at the level where the data are, delegates most operation decisions down the line and reserves for the executive those few broad policy decisions that shape the future of the enterprise. In the public sector, because of specialization and policy interests rather than managerial or operating interests, decisions tend to rise several levels above where the data are; policy decisions are often formulated at the mid-level with the executives often left with a crushing work load."

The separation of policy-making authority from implementation responsibility means that public managers more often are reacting to externally imposed change rather than managing changes that they have had a role in formulating. Public managers often have policy-making discretion. Nevertheless, they frequently find themselves reacting to policies set by others and, moreover, those policies change with great rapidity. One reason for change, as mentioned, is the cyclical nature of government. But also government seems more dominated (than is business) by crises. As one federal official put it, "It is not possible to set your own schedule. You can try, but you have to be ready to junk your whole schedule and go to whatever the crisis is" (Adams, 1979, p. 550). Public managers, like their business counterparts, sometimes can foresee crises. But more often they are dependent on others' perceptions of crises. In Washington, it is well known that a crisis occurs when Congress says a crisis has occurred (Lynn, 1981). Policy makers (in Congress and elsewhere) must first mobilize support for policies if anything is to be accomplished. One way to do this is to seize upon crises or even manufacture crises, thereby making their "cause" appear more urgent than others. This has two results: first, policy making proceeds in a herky-jerky fashion (responding to real or manufactured crisis); but, second, crisis policy making often reflects long-standing priorities that have been dormant, only awaiting the arrival of some set of events to animate them (Desai and Crow, 1983; Smart and Vertinsky, 1977). This means, then, that policy is dominated by crises but also that crisis-precipitated policies are not always formed as hurriedly as they appear to be.

Visibility. There are two stereotypes of public managers' visibility, each of which has some truth to it. There is the "invisible bureaucrat" buried deep in the bowels of bureaucracy and making seemingly anonymous decisions. But there is also the "life-in-a-goldfish-bowl" stereotype that envisions the public manager as someone whose every step is under the watchful eye of the mass media, constituents, interest groups, or political superiors.

The first stereotype is appropriate for many lower- and middle-level public managers, especially those operating in large agencies. They are likely to remain anonymous except in cases in which they are involved in enormous blunders, illegal acts, or whistle blowing. Most of what has been written about the high-profile, "constantly-in-the-public-eye" public manager has correctly focused on those at the highest levels. The question here is the extent to which the visibility of these public executives differs from that of business executives. Former Secretary of Defense James Forrestal offers one explanation as to why the public executive is more often a fixture in the print and broadcast media: "The difficulty of government work is that it not only has to be well done, but the public has to be convinced that it is being well done" (Lynn, 1981, p. 119). This explanation, which certainly has some validity, is based on the necessity that public executives "sell" their policies and programs to the public.

Even more important is the need for public accountability. Not only do the mass media have a "watchdog" function, but they also have a duty to keep the public informed about the flow of public events. No one really disputes the significance of this function, but there is an unceasing controversy about the limits of the public's need to know. Among the more hotly contested issues—which rarely affect private executives—are media coverage of the personal lives and families of public executives (Black, 1982; Anderson, 1970), the boundaries between accountability and open government on the one hand and the need for national security and executive privilege on the other (Levenson, 1978; Demac, 1984), and the proper timing for the release of information and the use of "leaked" information (Cathcart, 1984). These are complex issues that rarely constrain the activities of high-level business executives but are commonplace in the public sector. Another set of issues involving not only media relations but also legal requirements has to do with the public disclosure of officials' private finances—once again an issue that rarely affects business executives.

The Stakes. Business executives' policy decisions sometimes affect the lives of millions of citizens, but often the impacts are modest. Government policy decisions are more often broadly targeted, but, more important, the stakes are usually greater. Decisions involving the health, safety, and security of the public are routinely made by literally hundreds of government organizations each year. While the general public is sometimes greatly affected by the decisions of business enterprises, the number of policy actors and the number of "high-stakes" decisions produced by those actors are much smaller.

Even those government decisions that are narrow in scope are more likely to have significant impacts. Decisions by regulatory bodies, for example, may be directed at a party or parties that involve relatively few people; but the decision often has tremendous consequences for those whom it affects (Durant, 1986; Wilson and Rachal, 1977).

Comparisons of Organizations and Structures

At first blush, it might appear that the most straightforward and uncomplicated focus of comparison between public and private organizations would center on their respective structural attributes. Such is not the case. Studies comparing the structures of public organizations with those of private ones are uncommon, but studies of structure per se are plentiful. Hundreds of organization structure studies, most focusing on private organizations, have been produced, yet most critiques (Kimberly, 1976b; Dalton and others, 1980) have lamented the inconclusiveness and confusion of structure studies.

To illustrate the difficulty of comparing organizations' structures, let us consider the "uncomplicated" issue of organization size. In a review of the size literature, Kimberly (1976b) examined more than eighty empirical studies and observed that these studies encompassed only a fraction of the relevant literature. One of the reasons for the growth of this literature is apparent: size is, of course, an attribute shared by all organizations, and it is conveniently measured. But to say that size is conveniently measured is not to say that it is always consistently or even meaningfully measured. Researchers have measured size in terms of absolute number of employees, full-time personnel, authorized positions, gross receipts, size of annual budget, number of clients or customers, and indices combining these and other variables. Sometimes organization-specific measures are used, such as number of hospital beds or number of students. Sometimes size is studied across organizations, sometimes over time, and sometimes in research designs that consider the two simultaneously. Scores of studies have not provided a coherent picture. Studies examining the effects of size on performance have reported that size is not related to performance (Mahoney, Frost, Crandall, and Weitzel, 1972; Fiedler and Gillo, 1974); that size is positively related to performance (Reimann and Neghandhi, 1976); that size and performance are curvilinear (Herbst, 1957; Revans, 1958); and that size is related positively to some aspects of performance and negatively to others (Pugh, Hickson, Hinings, and Turner, 1968). Obviously, this covers most of the possibilities.

Considering that so many organization researchers have made so little progress studying so basic a structural attribute as size, the comparison of public and private organizations' structures seems a more formidable task than one might at first suppose.

Nevertheless, there are several studies that have provided some insight into the question of public-private structural differences.

Hood and Dunsire (1981) studied structural attributes of sixty-nine agencies of the British central government; although no comparable data were examined for nongovernment organizations, careful consideration was given by the authors to differences between their findings and those of a number of related studies (Aldrich, 1972; Child, 1973; Pugh, Hickson, and Hinings, 1969) of private-sector organizations. Traditional structural variables (such as differentiation, hierarchy, specialization, dispersion) were examined, as well as less standard structural variables, such as "diffraction" (the number of fringe units attached to an agency) and a variety of political status and influence variables ranging from number of bills introduced from an agency to number of parliamentary debates pertaining to an agency and its activities.

One of Hood and Dunsire's primary considerations was to determine whether agencies' structures could be predicted as a function of their technology, environment, and, especially, size. Contingency theorists (Blau and Schoenherr, 1971) have had some success predicting structure of private-sector organizations, and Hood and Dunsire, likewise, found regularities that could be interpreted on a similar basis. Particularly relevant to the publicness puzzle was the authors' investigation of the "iron grid effect": They reasoned that the civil service system and forces for centralization might reduce the variability of government agencies' structure and, thus, that size, technology, and environmental variables would be less significant as determinants of structure. No support for the iron grid effect was found among the larger agencies, which exhibited structural variation. However, among the smaller agencies there was much less variation in structure and the contingency variables were not useful in predicting structure.

Meyer's (1972, 1979) studies of the structure of state, local, and county finance and comptroller agencies provide the most detailed findings about the structure of government agencies in the United States. The most general conclusion from Meyer's interviews in more than 200 finance agencies is that the Weberian closed bureaucracy stereotype of the government agency is inappropriate and that "it may be that government agencies are properly more open to external pressures than popular beliefs about them would suggest" (Meyer, 1979, p. 14). But in addition to this overall conclusion, Meyer presents a number of more specific findings about the effects of structure in government agencies. Meyer (1979) found that increasing organizational size leads to elaboration of structure and structural complexity, a conclusion consistent with findings for private-sector organizations (Blau, Heydebrand, and Stauffer, 1966). Meyer's finding that bureaucratic formalization (measured by formalization of personnel procedures) leads to the elaboration of hierarchy is, however, at odds with findings which suggest that hierarchy leads to formalization (Hall, Haas, and Johnson, 1967). A particularly important conclusion in the Meyer study is that the structural configuration of government agencies has little independent relationship to organization effectiveness (although there are spurious relationships mediated by size and level of demand). This finding implies that attempts to achieve greater effectiveness through government reorganization and organization design may meet with little success.

One argument about differences in public and private organizations that is often advanced concerns longevity: It is alleged that government organizations have longer "life spans" because, among other reasons, they are sheltered from the vicissitudes of the marketplace. The best-known study of the longevity of government organizations is Herbert Kaufman's (1976) provocatively titled *Are Government Organizations Immortal?* Kaufman begins by reviewing the factors favoring longevity and those that threaten the existence of federal agencies. One factor favoring longevity is a basis in statute. Laws are not as easily changed as are administrative decisions, and if an act of Congress is required to abolish an agency, it is likely on safer ground. Developing patrons in Congress, a strategy employed by virtually every agency, is another aid to longevity. As agencies develop political exchange relationships with powerful members of Congress, they stand a better chance of survival even in the face of adversity. The budgetary process also favors the continuing existence of agencies. Despite the rhetoric of zero-based budgetary and similar devices, Congress does not have the capacity to perform a base-level review of every agency for each budget cycle.

There are important elements of incrementalism in the budgetary process. Incrementalism supports the status quo and, thus, the continuation of agencies. Furthermore, agencies assiduously cultivate clienteles, the public-sector counterpart of customers, to provide political support for their activities and, in some instances, to bear witness before appropriations committees that the agency's good works should continue to be sustained by the federal budget.

These potent forces for ensuring survival are not, of course, always sufficient to carry the day. Government agencies do go out of existence. Sometimes the factors that usually afford protection for an agency can threaten its existence. Just as a turtle's protective shell can prove a deadly encumbrance to a turtle turned on its back, so can the statutory basis and prescribed missions of agencies prove fatal. A firm experiencing diminishing demand for its product can diversify, develop new product lines, and pursue similarly adaptive strategies. While federal agencies are not always unable to expand functions and develop new clienteles, they are usually much more circumscribed than are firms. Furthermore, agencies usually find themselves in a competitive environment but with limited resources with which to compete. The competitive environment centers on political rather than market competition, but competition for budget shares, jurisdiction, and clienteles is crucial to agencies' survival. Perhaps most threatening, however, is a shift in political cycles. One administration's pet agency is the whipping boy of the next.

Kaufman's attempt to determine the longevity of federal agencies involved examination of data for 421 domestic agencies during the period 1923 to 1973. Although the study was undercut by severe problems in classification (name changes, program changes, reorganization), several patterns emerged nonetheless. It was found that the emergence of new agencies did not occur at a steady pace but proceeded in spurts. Somewhat surprisingly, a statutory basis appeared to provide little advantage over other forms of establishment. One important and controversial conclusion was that death rates, while significant, were substantially lower than among businesses. Nystrom and Starbuck (1981, p. 18) reinterpreted Kaufman's data and argued that "Kaufman biased his classifications toward demonstrating stability: he classified agencies as being lineal descendants even if they had different names, performed substantially different functions, belonged to different departments, and had no personnel in common with their ancestors." After applying a different analytical framework to federal agencies and corporations of similar size, Nystrom and Starbuck (1981, p. 21) conclude that "the similarity (in survival rates) between federal agencies and corporations is amazing . . . agencies and business firms appear about equally stable."

Conclusion

While the studies reviewed here have certainly begun to fit together some of the pieces of the publicness puzzle, there are more in the box than on the board. As we will see in Chapter Three, researchers have been hampered not by a lack of insight or imagination but by formidable problems related to data availability, access, sampling, and lack of financial support for research on publicness. Few studies go beyond simple comparison to provide causal hypotheses. Only a handful employ an integrated theoretical framework. In light of these handicaps, it is perhaps surprising that findings have shown some consistency. The fact that the publicness-privateness distinction emerges as important in studies that are highly diverse in design and intent indicates that it plays a crucial role in organization behavior.

3

Barriers to Developing
Knowledge About
the Publicness of
Organizations

Many of the problems that have plagued attempts to sort
out differences in public and private organizations are general
problems that confront virtually any effort to expand knowledge of
organizations and their behavior. There is little need to rehash
problems related directly to the state of the art in organizational
research ("general-purpose" critiques of organizational theory and
research are provided by Roberts, Hulin, and Rousseau, 1978, and
by Mohr, 1982). This chapter focuses on problems that are either
specific to research on public organizations or especially acute in
public organization research. For convenience, these problems are
grouped into four broad categories.

Four Obstacles to Understanding Public Organizations

Research and theory directed to the publicness puzzle have all
too often used ambiguous concepts measured haphazardly to provide unsatisfactory explanations of ephemeral phenomena. Respectively, the four elemental obstacles to public organization theory can
be categorized as analytical (ambiguous concepts), methodological (giving rise to haphazard measurement), causal (unsatisfactory
explanation), and synthetic (ephemeral phenomena).

The analytical problem is easily identified but not easily remedied. The term *publicness* has multiple meanings, nuances, and connotations. The methodological problem is many problems given a single label. It involves such matters as selecting the appropriate unit of analysis, choosing the most meaningful approach to aggregation, and developing research designs that are capable of sorting out the independent effects of publicness. The causal problem, at its most basic level, relates to the failure of many research studies to even suggest why public and private organizations (by whatever conceptualization) might be expected to behave differently. The synthetic problem deals with the changeability of the organizations themselves. The populations of organizations, as a result of changes in their function and character, present problems for the researcher. Hybrid and mixed-type organizations are increasing in number, and sector blurring is now rampant. This problem feeds back into the analytical problem, presenting added difficulty in the classification and measurement of the publicness of organizations. On the brighter side, the problems of public organization theory are epidemic, not pandemic. As discussed below, researchers and theorists have begun to make some progress.

The Synthetic Problem: The Blurring of Sectors

As Finney (1978, pp. 77-78) notes, "an either/or, public/private world, separating the government and for profit enterprises, has long ceased to exist, if it ever really did." Forces promoting the blurring of sectors are well known and require little discussion. Large corporations and even many small, family-owned businesses are dependent on government at their birth (for chartering, licensing, zoning), death (involving bankruptcy laws and merger and anti-trust policies), and points in between (regarding tax policies and resources from government contracts and loans). Government penetration of business firms is pervasive and of great significance (Committee for Economic Development, 1982).

At the same time, many government organizations are beginning to take on characteristics usually associated with business firms. A most obvious business-like practice is setting user charges (Straussman, 1981), but government agencies are increasingly becoming involved in advertising and marketing (Yarwood and Enis, 1982; Kotler and Sidney, 1969; Bozeman and Straussman, 1983) and "business-like" approaches to compensation (Smith, 1982; Wheat, 1982), collective bargaining (Shaw and Clark, 1972), and financial management (Methe, Baesel, and Schulman, 1983).

A development related to the convergence of business and government organizations' attributes and practices is the rise of hybrid organizations which are partly public and partly private. The government enterprise is a major variety of hybrid organization (Walsh, 1978). There is much variation in the structure, legal status, and functions of government enterprises, but in virtually every instance they serve to make traditional public-private distinctions even more tenuous.

Government-sponsored enterprises (GSEs) and multi-organization enterprises (MOEs) are two hybrids that have contributed to the ambiguity of public-private distinctions. Since 1960, the proliferation of GSEs has been extensive, with not fewer than twenty-five having been established by the United States Congress alone. These organizations are difficult to classify, in part because a GSE can have any of the following legal statuses: (1) private, for-profit corporation; (2) government-sponsored private corporation; (3) wholly owned government enterprise; (4) private nonprofit corporation; (5) multi-organization enterprise; (6) public corporation; (7) independent establishment; and/or (8) United States instrumentality. This multiplicity of legal statuses, along with varied operating procedures and funding sources, defies conventional classification. In some cases, the GSEs compete in the marketplace; in other cases, they do not permit competition.

In Europe, where GSEs are even more prolific, Mazzolini (1979) has shown that these types of organizations are distinctive in two important ways. First, in the resource acquisition phase, GSEs are able to obtain greater funding and assume greater risk than non-GSEs operating in the same business sector. In addition, labor relations in GSEs have proved to be an obstacle to achievement of financial goals.

The MOE is often a structural response to tasks or problems that are large scale and technologically based (Horwitch, 1979). The development of MOEs appears to occur in those areas in which a single organization is unable technically, financially, politically, or managerially to handle the entire project. Recent examples include: Super Phoenix Breeder Project (France); synthetic fuels development in the United States; European space development and the development of the SST. Horwitch and Prahalad (1981) have identified five major characteristics generally exhibited by MOEs: (1) mission orientation; (2) conglomeration of organizations with diverse organizational cultures, motivations, and goals; (3) both private and public organizations participate; (4) organizational homes of MOE members generally continue to maintain separate identity; and (5) MOEs are almost always large, complex organizations requiring resources from all members. The expanded use of MOE structures to address new problems further promotes blurring of traditional public-private distinctions.

While in many instances it is still possible to identify and compare a set of "core public" and "core private" organizations, there is need for theory that deals head-on with the blurring of sectors, the penetration of private organizations by government, the business-like attributes of government organizations, and the ambiguous legal status of hybrid organizations.

The Analytical Problem: Conceptualizing "Public" Organizations

One of the most formidable obstacles to the resolution of the publicness puzzle is the ambiguity of such terms as *public organization, public service,* and even *governmental.* Theorists and researchers often use these terms not only in a manner that is inconsistent with the uses of others but sometimes in a way that is internally inconsistent. The ambiguities are not simply a result of carelessness in the use of concepts. Many aspects of the behavior of public organizations seem to demand the modifier "public" (Benn and Gaus, 1983). Some of the more familiar uses of the term are briefly discussed below.

Public-as-Government. Often the term *public organization* is used to refer to government organizations; it is descriptive of the formal legal status of an organization. This is one of the more meaningful uses of the term for purposes of conducting research, and many of the comparative public-private studies (for example, Rainey, 1979; Buchanan, 1975a) use the term in this way. One problem with this conceptualization is that it typically makes no distinction among nongovernment organizations, and thus it fails to deal with possible differences between, say, business firms and not-for-profit organizations. Likewise, this conceptualization is poorly equipped to deal with mixed-type organizations such as government enterprises or multi-organization forms.

Despite its limitations, the public-as-government conceptualization has much to recommend it to researchers and theorists. Rainey, Backoff, and Levine (1976) argue cogently that research comparing public and private organizations can advance by identifying "core sets" of government organizations and contrasting them to core sets of business organizations and, at least for the time being, paying little heed to the more complicated and less easily classified mixed-type. And there is more than measurement convenience to support the use of the public-as-government conceptualization. It seems likely that most people already think in these terms. Policy makers' discussions of public and private sectors usually seem to imply a "core business," "core government" connotation.

Public-as-Economic-Character. There is a well-developed body of concepts from economics dealing with the public aspects of organizations. Here the emphasis is not on the legal status of the organization but on such issues as whether a good or service provided by the organization is exclusionary (whether it is possible to levy user charges), whether there is a market for the goods or services produced by the organization, whether one person's consumption of the good has an effect on the amount available for others, whether there are significant externalities or spillover effects, and whether the good or service is most efficiently financed by a collective rather than by individuals. Significantly, economists have noted that few organizations' products and services are purely public or purely private.

The public-as-economic-character concept has been highly influential in policy making and in certain branches of organization theory (see, for example, Breton and Winetrobe, 1982; Williamson, 1981b; Mitnick, 1979). It has several advantages, not the least of which is that publicness is not viewed as a discrete variable but as a dimensional property and thus complications arising from sector blurring and mixed-type organizational forms are more easily addressed. Nevertheless, there are some limitations. In the first place, the concepts of public choice theorists are more often used (and more easily applied) in normative analysis than for describing observed organization behavior. Furthermore, a focus on the economic character of the organizations' goods and services (to the exclusion of other important aspects of organizations) is limiting.

Public-as-Public-Interest. There is much confusion surrounding the notion of public interest. But the fact that public interest is such a hopelessly ambiguous term does not lessen its importance. Often public organizations are viewed as those working in or serving the public interest, and it has been argued that one of the most basic features distinguishing public from private organizations is public awareness of and stake in the organization's activity (Goodsell, 1983; Gusfield, 1981).

Noting the ambiguities entailed in various uses of the term *public interest,* Shubert (1957) suggests that the concept has outlived its usefulness and should be abandoned. Yet despite the ambiguities that seem to be inherent, the concept is widely used and remains important not only in academic circles but in public policy discussions as well. Statutes are written instructing agencies to regulate "in the public interest," and business and professional organizations (such as physicians' review boards) are sometimes accorded special-interest status and powers because they are judged as acting in the public interest. Furthermore, the general public seems to have different expectations for organizations (government and nongovernment) that conduct activities deemed to be in the public interest (Redford, 1965; Vogel, 1975). While the effects of public expectations on organizations' behavior are not easily traced, neither are they easily discounted.

Normative and Ideological Confusion. Discussions of publicness are confused not only by a lack of conceptual clarity but also by the mixing of normative, value-laden usage with descriptive and denotative usage. Even the public-as-government usage is sometimes muddled by the diverse connotations of the term. In discussions of publicness, ideological views often become entangled with descriptions.

One illustration of a normative theme that sometimes has confused efforts to sort out differences between public and private organizations is the "business-like government" theme. This theme's roots can be traced back to the beginnings of the nation, but it remains important in contemporary deliberations. Part of the confusion engendered by ideological filters is that they have different meanings to different people. But if there is any common thread running through business-like government views, it is an emphasis on efficiency. Indeed, government reforms from the Hoover Commission to the Grace Commission, from Robert McNamara's Department of Defense (DOD) "whiz kid" efficiency experts to President Reagan's business braintrust, have been concerned with promoting efficiency in government. To many, government is most business-like when it is efficient. By the same token, government is least business-like when it is political. Often attempts to run government like a business have led to reform movements aimed at lessening the influence of partisan and constituency politics or separating politics from administration (Kaufman, 1956).

It may appear that economic efficiency is a nonideological issue that anyone could easily support. Likewise, it might seem, especially to business-like government proponents, that the elimination of politics in favor of greater economic efficiency is a step that only the most irrational or self-interested would oppose. To be sure, the idea that politics (at least constituency and electoral politics) is the enemy of efficiency is at least a partial truth. If efficiency is the production of a given unit of output with a minimum of input, politics is often antithetical to efficiency.

However, if efficiency is the minimization of waste, the relationship of politics to efficiency is not so clear. Politics is less often a source of waste than an additional (that is, noneconomic) set of allocational criteria (Fitch, 1974). Claims of equity, redistribution of resources, and regulation of hazardous practices and products often conflict with efficiency objectives. The call for efficiency in government and, sometimes, more business-like government is often accompanied by unarticulated but powerful ideological assumptions. To the extent that having business-like government means tipping the scales from political "efficiency" to economic efficiency, business-like government will often serve elite interests (Schiesl, 1977). Likewise, business-like government (again meaning economically efficient) is more likely to enhance the role of professional public managers and technicians and undermine the influence of elected officials (Dutton and Kraemer, 1977; Rose, 1977; Olsen, 1979).

The business-like government theme is only one example of the intrusion of normative and ideological filters into attempts to sort out empirical differences between public and private organizations. This is not to say, of course, that value issues are unimportant in discussion of public and private organizations—only that care must be taken not to allow notions about how organizations should behave to confuse analysis of how they do behave. Some normative perspectives, such as public choice theory, can help clarify thinking about actual behavioral differences among organizations and can serve as a source of hypotheses. Other normative perspectives do more to confuse than to clarify. For example, the normative strain of the business-like government issue is often little more than a red herring for organization theorists; the controversy obscures theoretical issues and contributes little to their resolution. Even as an empirical issue, running government like a business is usually a slogan or a political symbol (and often an important one). Just what does it mean to run government like a business? Herbert Hoover sought business-like government in the 1920s, and so has Ronald Reagan in the 1980s. But it seems likely that being "business-like" might mean something different today from what it meant in Hoover's time. Consider the significance of such developments as the rise of the modern corporation and the multinational corporation, the separation of ownership from management, the "professionalization" of management, the shift to a service-dominated economy, government regulation of business, reliance on information and communication technology—all these factors have altered business institutions and business practice. Even the meaning and the role of profit have changed.

The Methodological Problem: Measurement and Construct Validity Issues

It is not surprising, in light of the multiple meanings of publicness and the changes in the actual composition of organizations and sectors, that researchers concerned with the publicness puzzle have encountered problems in developing useful constructs, measures, and measurement approaches. Some of the more common problems are reviewed here.

Coding. Often such a fundamental issue as developing a coding scheme for public organizations proves to be a nearly insurmountable task. This is well illustrated by Hood and Dunsire's (1981) efforts. Their attempt to determine characteristics of British government agencies was nearly thwarted at the very beginning because of difficulties in determining which agencies should be viewed as autonomous units and which should be viewed as subunits. In order to develop a preliminary list of autonomous government agencies, Hood and Dunsire consulted several authoritative sources, including personnel documents, budget documents, content-analyzed references in the deliberations of Parliament, civil service statistics, and discussions with ministers and senior public managers. Among the thirty-five government agencies examined, more than half were omitted from at least one source list; there was no consensus, then, as to which agencies were autonomous entities. Their conclusion: "It is perhaps futile to debate what constitutes a significant level of organization in abstracto; significance may vary with the particular problem that is being addressed at any one time" (Hood and Dunsire, 1981, p. 38).

It is worth observing that classification problems are not unique to analysis of public organizations (McKelvey, 1982; Pinder and Moore, 1979). It is not always a simple matter to determine whether business organizations are best viewed as autonomous units or as subsidiaries. Nevertheless, the problems are less acute when dealing with business organizations because the formal interdependencies are fewer, wide-scale reorganizations are less common, and there is no direct equivalent of the changes in budgetary processes that affect the government organization's status and character. Also, as Kaufman (1976) has noted, it is more difficult to determine "birth" dates and termination dates of government organizations. Does a government organization come into existence when it is given statutory authorization (some agencies given statutory authorization receive no funds, hire no one, and carry out no activities), when budget and personnel are authorized, when the agency receives its funds, or when it begins to provide services?

Level of Analysis. There are two different level-of-analysis problems that must be reckoned with in research comparing public and private organizations. Among other possibilities, studies comparing public and private organizations (and public and private management) can examine the behavior of individuals, groups of individuals, whole organizations, sets of organizations, and sectors. There is no reason to believe that the effects of publicness would be the same at each level or that one would find differences among public and private actors at each level (Lerner, 1986). Thus, a study focusing on the differences in goal-directed behaviors of public and private managers (a study at the individual level of analysis) might come to quite different conclusions from those of a study that examines the differences in the goal-directed behavior of whole organizations (at the organizational level of analysis). This seems an obvious point, but the literature describing alleged differences in public and private organizations often glosses over this distinction and proceeds to compare studies at different levels of analysis.

There is another level-of-analysis problem that has similarly important consequences for making sense out of comparisons of public and private organizations and managers: studies focus on managers at different levels in the organizational hierarchy. It should come as no surprise that studies focusing on top executives have found more differences than similarities between those in government and business, whereas those focusing on middle-level managers and below have found fewer differences. Nevertheless, reviews of the literature often fail to distinguish between studies of top management and studies of middle- and lower-level employees, thus further complicating our understanding of publicness.

Aggregation. Organization researchers are confronted with a host of measurement problems pertaining to aggregation (Freeman, 1978). Nowhere are aggregation problems more troubling than in efforts to sort out differences between public and private organizations. At high levels of aggregation, it is more likely that general patterns will emerge and that particular organizations can be assessed against these general patterns. But at lower levels of aggregation (the single organization taken as the lowest), the unique properties of individual organizations become more apparent. It is not surprising, then, that persons focusing on single organizations are more likely sensitive to the unique properties of those organizations and that persons who aggregate organizations are more sensitive to patterned behavior. However, reviews of the literature comparing public and private organizations sometimes fail to distinguish systematically among studies at different levels of aggregation. Case studies of a single organization are considered along with studies of hundreds of organizations. We might expect that persons working at different levels of aggregation would come to different conclusions regarding the significance of publicness and that these conclusions might be due in large part to the level of aggregation. Among those studies that have found significant differences in public organizations, the case study is a common methodology. However, studies finding few significant differences on the basis of publicness have most often looked at large numbers of organizations and have tended to aggregate organization behaviors. In sum, if one focuses on the unique, one finds the unique; if one focuses on groups, one finds patterns and common behavior.

Organizers, Organizing, and Organizations. It is important to maintain distinctions among organizers (the people working in organizations), organizing (managing), and the organizations themselves. Again, this seems a simple enough point, but discussions of public-private differences often go back and forth between different foci without noting the change. To say that there are differences between public and private organizations is not the same as saying that there are differences between public and private managers or between public and private management. This is not unlike Weick's (1969) argument about the significance of organizing to the study of organizations.

The Causal Problem: The Ultimate Barrier to Public Organization Theory

Even if the other major problems are solved, even if appropriate constructs and methods are developed, little progress is possible in the absence of some useful explanation of how publicness affects the behavior of organizations. It is not enough to determine that public organizations (by some conception) differ in their behaviors from private organizations. Some explanation of just how the publicness of organizations affects their behavior is a requirement for significant advances in theory. Currently, research on public organizations relies all too often on "blackbox empiricism" (Bozeman, 1982) or ad hoc explanation.

The dimensional theory of publicness (developed in Chapters Four, Five, and Six) seeks to provide a conceptual advance in that it enables one to deal with sector blurring, hybrid organizations, and interrelationships among diverse organization types. But the more ambitious goal is to provide a plausible explanation as to just how the publicness of organization affects behaviors. It attempts, in short, to outline the behavioral mechanics of publicness. The approach presented here is best understood in relation to other approaches to understanding differences between public and private organizations. The next section presents a typology of predominant approaches to the publicness puzzle.

Approaches to the Publicness Puzzle

Previous chapters review empirical findings and theories pertaining to publicness without systematically characterizing approaches. It is useful to briefly categorize general approaches (apart from substantive findings) to the study of public organizations. There is considerable diversity in approaches to the analysis of publicness of organizations (Rainey, Backoff, and Levine, 1976; Bozeman, 1984). Despite the diversity, it is possible to capture most of the more common approaches to publicness in just a few categories.

Practitioner accounts have played a prominent role in framing the publicness puzzle. Especially useful is the work of "sector spanners" (persons working in high-level positions in both government and business), who provide accounts of observed differences in public and private organizations and management. Classic studies by Wilson (1887) and Appleby (1945) remain valuable, and more recent sector spanners such as Blumenthal (1983) and Rumsfeld (1979) offer impressions about similarities and differences in public and private organizations. While these accounts are suggestive and often a fruitful source of hypotheses (see, for example, Allison, 1979), their prominence in theoretical discussions of differences in public and private organizations is testimony to the paucity of systematic empirical research comparing public and private organizations.

Case studies comparing public and private organizations are uncommon, but there is an extensive literature focusing on single public organizations (for example, Selznick, 1966; Mosher, 1979). Many of these studies make no claim to deal with differences between public and private organizations, but others (such as Warwick, 1975; Kaufman, 1981) use their case material to make inferences about differences. It is likely that a carefully matched set of case studies of public and private organizations could shed much light on the publicness puzzle, but it appears that no one has undertaken such a systematic comparison of cases. Studies focusing on single organizations, or unsystematically on several organizations, are often useful in teaching but only rarely make an important contribution to theory of public organizations.

In *single-sector research,* the investigator examines a sample of public organizations (or subunits of public organizations), determines the empirical characteristics of the organization, and uses this information to speculate about differences between public and private organizations. A familiar example of this approach is Meyer's (1979) *Change in Public Bureaucracies.* Meyer provides strong arguments about the need to pay attention to differences in public and private organizations and cautions against overgeneralization in organization theory but provides no empirical comparison of public and private organizations. In perhaps the most thoroughgoing attempt to define the characteristics of public organizations, Hood and Dunsire (1981) have taken the lead in providing empirically derived definitions. But, again, comparison with private organizations is either implicit or speculative, as there is no similar data base for private organizations.

Comparative sector research seems to hold much promise as a basis for theories of public organization. Unfortunately, while such studies are beginning to accumulate (for example, Buchanan, 1974, 1975a; Meyer, Marshall, and Williams, 1977; Rainey, 1983, 1979; Rushing, 1973; Bozeman and Loveless, forthcoming; Crow, 1985), they are sometimes flawed by such problems as nonsystematic sampling and other data limitations, misspecification of models, and limited construct validity. Some of the more rigorous studies (such as Rhinehart and others, 1969) have been laboratory based and have employed students as subjects. The generalizability of such studies is questionable.

Generic research is the most common in organization studies. In generic research, there is no presumption that differences between public and private organizations are significant. In such studies, government, not-for-profit, and business organizations may be taken together, but (at least in terms of publicness) "an organization is an organization." In a variant, which might be referred to as *incidental publicness research,* sector status is investigated but plays a minor role in the analysis (see, for example, Rushing, 1976; Holdaway, Newberry, Hickson, and Heron, 1975; Rowan, 1982; Tolbert and Zucker, 1983). In such cases, typically no theoretical justification is given for observed differences between public and private organizations. Publicness is examined more or less as an afterthought.

Finally, there are studies that resemble the approach taken here—studies that seek to develop *theoretical frameworks* to address the publicness puzzle. Some of these studies (such as Fottler, 1981; Wamsley and Zald, 1973) are rooted in the traditions of organization theory, but other useful approaches are firmly anchored in the disciplines of political science (for instance, Benn and Gaus, 1983) or economics (for example, Breton and Winetrobe, 1982). Many of the conceptual models are a rich source of testable hypotheses, but with the exception of the property rights framework of economists, these "pre-theories" have received insufficient attention from researchers. One reason, perhaps, for the apparent neglect is that the conceptual models tend to deal with the organization-environment interactions, whereas researchers concerned with the publicness puzzle have chiefly examined the role of individuals in organizations.

A Typology of Approaches

To summarize, we have identified seven reasonably distinct approaches to publicness: practitioner accounts, case studies, single-sector research (implicit comparisons), comparative sector research, generic research, incidental publicness research, and theoretical frameworks. It is possible to develop from these approaches a crude typology that sorts out approaches on the basis of (1) whether they seek generalizations and (2) whether they aggregate or separate public and private organizations.

Ideographic Approaches to the Publicness Puzzle. Ideographic approaches seek to explain singular events, often in a developmental context. Such studies do provide an explanation of sorts, but they rely heavily on the analyst's interpretative ability rather than on inferences drawn systematically from data. Graham (1971, p. 201) notes that ideographic approaches can provide an "explanation sketch" but cautions that "every sketch can be written differently if one emphasizes the effects of one variable within the context over others . . . how does one compare contextual explanations (even those adopting the same perspective) in order to judge whether one is more accurate or valid than another?" Practitioner accounts and case studies are ideographic in their approach to explanation and, while useful in many ways, have little potential for valid generalization. Indeed, practitioner accounts can sometimes mislead those seeking general explanations of differences between public and private organizations and their management.

Practitioners writing books and articles about differences in public- and private-sector organizations are hardly a random lot. The more familiar first-hand accounts are those written by officials working with the highest levels of government and business. Not only are these individuals far from representative of all managers, but it is unlikely that they represent all managers at the highest levels. There is no reason to expect that sector spanners would be a randomly distributed sample of all upper-level managers.

Not all case studies are atheoretical. But case studies that do not concern themselves with the generation of hypotheses or with the matching of public and private organizations are atheoretical (at least in respect to the publicness question). Studies that simply assume that public- and private-sector organizations are different and proceed to investigate the behavior of a single organization on the basis of that assumption would qualify as ideographic case studies of publicness.

Generalization-Seeking Approaches to the Publicness Puzzle: Aggregate Versus Binary. Most generic, incidental publicness, single-sector, comparative sector, and theoretical framework approaches can be classed as theoretical in that each seeks generalizable explanation of organization behavior. These approaches can be further subdivided according to whether they aggregate or separate public and private organizations. The term *binary* describes the treatment of publicness in most comparative sector and single-sector studies. They are binary in the sense that organizations are separated into one of two categories (public versus private ownership, public sector versus private sector, government versus business, market versus nonmarket). In the case of single-sector studies, the distinctions are not based on empirical

Figure 3.1. A Typology of Approaches to Publicness in Organization Research

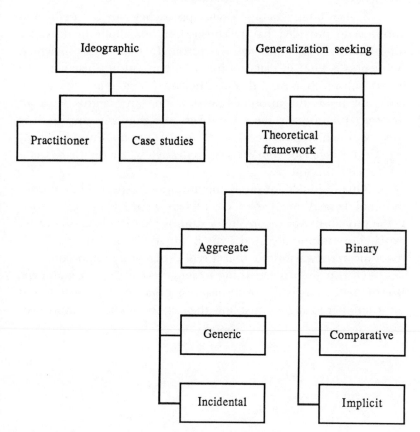

comparisons but rather are implicit. That is, one presents findings for one set (for example, the public sector) of organizations.

Aggregate approaches make no such distinction. Instead, organizations are taken together without consideration of publicness. Both the generic and incidental publicness approaches are essentially aggregate in that "an organization is an organization" (at least in regard to public/private status).

Figure 3.1 presents a typology of approaches based on their type of explanation (ideographic and generalization seeking) and the manner in which they deal (or choose not to deal) with publicness.

Either binary or aggregate approaches can be useful and appropriate, provided that the core assumption about the relevance (or irrelevance) of publicness is correct. In those cases in which publicness is vital in determining an organization's behavior, the binary approach is useful and efficient. When that assumption does not hold, the approach wastes time and begins with an incorrect premise. By the same token, the aggregate approach is successful when publicness is of modest or no importance in explaining behavior, but it is less effective when publicness is a critical determinant.

One rationale for public organization theory is the minimization of Type A and Type B error where Type A (aggregate) error is the probability of incorrectly assuming that publicness is of no explanatory importance and Type B (binary) error is the probability of incorrectly assuming that it is of explanatory importance.

Of course, it is one thing to suggest that Type A and Type B error reduction is a worthy task for organization research and quite another to suggest just how the task should be accomplished.

4

Economic Authority: Understanding the Roots of Privateness

Authority exists "whenever one, several, or many people explicitly or tacitly permit someone else to make decisions for them for some category of acts" (Lindblom, 1977, pp. 17–18). The behavioral consequent of authority is compliance, and the study of authority in organizations is, at least in part, an inquiry into the reasons for compliance to formal organizational directives.

Economic authority is a powerful motivator in organizations of virtually every type. Individuals comply with organizational directives in hopes of receiving pecuniary reward. Economic authority is not the sole means at the disposal of the organization: Compliance also can be explained as a function of commitment to religious dogma (religious and clerical authority), ideology (authority of ideas), and charisma (authority of personality). But most modern organizations are nourished by economic and political authority, and this analysis is restricted to these two broad categories of authority. The focus here and in the next chapter is on the uses and impacts of organizational authority in environmental transactions. The reader interested in exploring the dynamics of political and economic authority within organizations will find several useful explanations in the existing literature (see Breton and Winetrobe, 1982; Downs, 1967; Hoenack, 1983).

Note: This chapter was written with Stephen Loveless and draws from Loveless, 1985, and Bozeman and Loveless, forthcoming.

Economic Authority and Publicness

The virtues of selfishness have long been recognized by economists. Concern with economic self-interest is a driving force in a capitalistic economy and, more important for present purposes, a cornerstone of economic authority. Economic self-interest is a prerequisite for inducing compliance in market-based organizations. Even the most simplistic interpretations of public-private distinctions readily identify one significant factor: presence or absence of a profit motive. Cruder interpretations are content to note that there's no "bottom line" in government. But sophisticated treatments recognizing the many complexities in meaning and effect of profit motives provide the same elemental lesson. However, economists disagree on the relevance of the profit motive as a distinction between public and private organizations. This is due in part to the widespread recognition that few organizations, public or private, are driven solely by profit motives. And it is due in part to divergent opinions about the role of government in a capitalistic society.

One view of the role of government, a "minimalist" model, is as a support for the marketplace. Perhaps the leading advocate of this model of government action is Milton Friedman (1984), who argues that the sphere of government activity should be limited to defining and reinforcing ownership, specifying criminal behavior and liabilities, and removing barriers to competition (such as anti-trust legislation). According to this view, the role of the government is to maintain competition and, thus, consumer sovereignty.

A much more aggressive role for government is argued by economic planners such as Galbraith (1967), who argues that the character of industrial technology and production is such that many alternative suppliers are not desirable because of scale economies. Efficient use of modern technology requires considerable ability to anticipate change, and this in turn requires greater planning than is possible in an unfettered market environment. While planning in private corporations ensures some ability to anticipate change, such planning is atomistic and nondemocratic and an expanded government role is required for fuller participation in anticipation and management of change.

It seems fair to suggest that the dominant model of government action is the market failure model. This model identifies several factors that prevent the efficient operation of the market (Samuelson, 1966). But whereas the minimalist model restricts government activity to promotion of competition, the market failure model suggests that certain activities are better performed by the government because of exclusion costs, transactions costs, or free-rider features present in market provision of goods or services. The market failure model underpins much of the reasoning of public goods, public choice, and public expenditure theory. Many of the assumptions of the market failure model color another body of economic theory relevant to publicness—property rights theory.

Market failure and property rights theories provide the grist for an interpretation of the implications of economic authority for publicness. Property rights theory is especially fruitful for understanding differences in public and private organizations. Whereas much of the market failure literature is essentially normative and deals with guidelines for allocating duties among sectors, property rights theory not only considers allocational criteria but also offers an explanation of observed differences in the behavior and productivity of public and private organizations.

Market failure can occur in cases in which monopolies or oligopolies exist. Government action is the usual tool for dealing with the resultant breakdowns in competition. Those actions may be aimed at either correcting the market or providing goods or services through government agencies. In some instances, the market can establish costs and facilitate exchange but transaction costs are prohibitively expensive. For example, it is possible to levy direct charges on pedestrians for the use of sidewalks, but it is certainly impractical. The transaction costs are such that the market is not efficient.

The market failure criterion is not as straightforward as it might seem. Market imperfections almost always exist to some degree. The prime question, then, is not whether there is a market failure but whether it is sufficient to warrant government action. Also, it is a mistake to compare delivery of goods and services by inefficient markets with delivery by some ideally efficient government actor. Wolf (1979) has cogently argued that one must consider the possibilities of "nonmarket failure." Such factors as power inequities, displacement of public goals by private goals, and the inability to control cost can foil nonmarket delivery of goods and services.

Public Goods

According to some economic theorists, goods and services should be provided by public-sector organizations when there are market imperfections or when the goods and services can themselves be classified as public goods. There are several extant definitions of public goods. Some economists refer to all goods and services provided by government via indirect financing (that is, taxation and appropriations) as public goods. This is not an especially helpful definition, because it centers on mode of financing rather than on the character of the goods themselves. Herber (1971, p. 32) provides a more conventional definition centering on exclusion and joint consumption characteristics of the goods: "The primary characteristic of collective consumption is the fact that 'jointly consumed' economic goods are indivisible in the important sense that some or all of their benefits cannot be priced in the market. In the extreme case of all benefits being indivisible, the good is normally called a 'pure public good.' If such a good is supplied in the economy, it is consumed in an equal amount by all consumers. No one can be 'excluded' from its consumption by a failure to voluntarily pay for it."

While public goods character is a criterion prescribed by many economists for determining allocation of responsibilities between sectors, few goods and services qualify as purely public. National defense is an often-cited example of pure public good: It is as available to pacifists as to hawks; once it is provided to one, it is provided to all; and one person's consumption does not diminish the amount available to others. But most of the goods and services provided by government fall somewhere between purely private character (that is, divisible, exclusionary, conveniently priced in the market) and purely public character. Also a good may be more public in some of its aspects and less so in others. James Buchanan (1973) has given extensive theoretical treatment to so-called quasi-public goods.

For the purpose of locating an activity in the public or the private sector, the relative convenience with which a price can be set for the goods or services is usually a major issue. One consideration is the presence and extent of externalities. Externalities arise when some value (positive or negative) of a good or service is not reflected in its price or resources used. Examples of externalities include the production of air pollutants by manufacturers and the social (as opposed to the individual) value of formal education. Often policy makers seek to manage externalities (for example, by regulating producers of pollution and subsidizing individuals' education).

The pure public good is an extreme case of externalities in that all of the output is viewed as unmarketable to individuals because all of the benefits are external. Thus, one criterion for location of a good or service in the public sector is the generation of significant positive externalities. By the same token, if all the benefits accrue to the individual, an efficient market structure is possible, meaningful prices can be set, and the production of the good or service should theoretically be the responsibility of the private sector. This criterion is not as clear-cut as it might seem, however, since there is much variance in the amount and type of externalities associated with particular goods and services. Just as there are few purely public goods, there are few for which benefits are entirely external.

Public goods approaches have been influential not only in the development of economic approaches to organization theory (see, for example, Breton and Winetrobe, 1982; Downs, 1967; Williamson, 1981a) but also in guiding public policy decisions. However, public goods and market failure approaches are not emphasized in this chapter. The chief concern here is not with *prescribing* differences between public and private organizations but with *explaining* differences in behavior and performance.

Property Rights as a Theory of Publicness

In addition to public goods and market failure criteria for distinguishing public- and private-sector organizations and their activities, economists have developed arguments pertaining to property rights and ownership (Alchian and Demsetz, 1972; Alchian, 1965; De Alessi, 1969, 1973, 1980; Demsetz, 1966, 1967). According to property rights theorists, the most important distinction between private and government organizations lies in the inability to transfer the rights of ownership in government organizations from one individual or group to another. Since there are no shares of government stock, the individual cannot alter his or her "portfolio" of investments in government programs or exchange ownership rights. There are several important economic implications of this inability to transfer ownership rights. It is argued (Alchian, 1961; Peltzman, 1971) that the ability to exchange ownership is related to economic efficiency. Economists view ownership as a productive input that functions to bear risk and organize managerial activity (Peltzman, 1971). In public organizations, risk (at least capital risk) is diffused to such a degree that it virtually ceases to exist (Cheung, 1969). An implication of the private sector's treatment of management as a productive input is that ability tends to be efficiently valued in the market; in the public sector, the distribution of managerial ability among organizations has little correspondence to its value as a productive input (Jensen and Meckling, 1976; Clarkson, 1980).

Reward and Incentives. When ownership rights are transferable, there is a clear connection between decision and reward. In the absence of property rights, there is additional inefficiency related to the fact that bureaucratic regulations and monitoring mechanisms are promulgated as an inadequate but costly substitute for valuations and reward systems based on property rights (Alchian and Demsetz, 1973). Such controls include nepotism, tenure, salary structures, sealed bids, and line item budget controls (Davies, 1981)—none of which is necessary when owners have pecuniary incentives to strive for efficiency.

In the absence of direct financial stakes, the mission of the public agency is more easily subverted. Consider Bower's (1977, p. 132) observation about the dilution of purpose in the public sector: "What does *purpose* mean in the public sector? As in the private sector, the administration motive is self-interest; but the stated organizational motive is *not*. . . . The administrator who finds a 'product' to keep the Rural Electrification Administration alive is criticized as a recalcitrant bureaucrat, a preserver of unneeded jobs. Though it may motivate administrative success, self-interest is venal. Moreover, the chief executive in a public organization may have no presumptive right to set purpose; it may be given by legislation."

Owner-Entrepreneur Oversight. Government organizations do not benefit from the services of wealth-seeking entrepreneurs. Even if entrepreneurs were successful in initiating or restructuring government organizations for maximal productivity, there is no mechanism by which the entrepreneurs benefit more than other taxpayers and there is no guarantee that taxes will be reduced as a result of increased efficiency. Nor is there much prospect for individual taxpayers to be rewarded for time spent monitoring government action and seeking efficiency. The activist taxpayer benefits no more than others. In private firms, entrepreneurs and wealth-sharing managers exert pressure for the combination of economic input that maximizes productivity. In government, managerial activity centers around more diverse rationales (Shelton, 1967; Clarkson, 1980), particularly side payments related to political power, budget expansions, and increments in personnel (Downs, 1967; Niskanen, 1971). As Davies (1981, p. 115) notes, lacking such binding constraints as pressure to maximize owners' wealth, "a public manager will have great opportunity to increase his well-being at the expense of the owners' [that is, taxpayers'] wealth to a greater extent than a manager of a proprietary concern because it is relatively less costly to do so."

A related point is introduced by Alchian and Demsetz (1972), who seek to explain "shirking." Market forces conduce coordination and meaningful evaluation of work. In the absence of market forces, the individual public employee, who values not only productivity but also leisure and other personal objectives, will have motivation to shift the work burden to others (shirk). The cost of any individual's reduced productivity is borne by the entire group, while the gain in nonproductive value is his or hers alone.

In order to combat shirking, the work group must be closely monitored. The importance of proprietary property rights in the firm is to provide the means and the motivation for monitoring activity. Under owner control, the right to residual profits and the right to transfer or sell ownership provide the incentive to maximize the organization's productivity and long-term net value. Likewise, owner control provides the means of monitoring. The owner(s) has the right to observe and assess work, hire and fire employees, and serve as the central party to contracts. Thus, in the view of Alchian and Demsetz (1972), the cluster of proprietary rights in the classic free enterprise firm has evolved as the most effective means of ensuring that shirking is held to a minimum and that technical efficiency is optimized.

Monitoring in Government Organizations and the Modern Corporation. As ownership becomes attenuated—diluted among many owners—the motivation and means of direct owner control also become diluted. This is as true in the large modern corporation as it is in the public organization. But in the modern corporation more effective means are available to combat the loss of owner control and its undesirable consequences (De Alessi, 1973). The most important technique is the delegation of monitoring to a smaller group of managers or manager-owners. The managers are motivated to serve as owner-surrogates in cases in which the managers' income is tied to the organization's profit and capital value. Also, the managers' tenure is in part a function of the organization's success (as defined by the owner-shareholders).

Both conditions are enabled by the ability to freely transfer ownership shares. Open trading of ownership shares allows easy assessment of the organization's value and, consequently, of links between managerial reward and performance (Di Lorenzo and Robinson, 1982). Further, the right to transfer ownership shares establishes the possibility of the inefficient organization changing hands and the manager being replaced.

The key differences between the stereotypical public organization and the corporation are the nontransferable nature of ownership, the consequential inability of public owners (taxpayers) to accumulate additional shares, and restrictions on the distribution of residual benefits.

Ownership in the public organization is not voluntary. The owner of the public organization can escape ownership only by moving—he or she cannot sell or transfer his or her share. As a consequence, the owner's ability to collect the benefits of the organization's increased wealth and future income is considerably reduced, as is the owner's incentive to monitor. Potential for takeover by a new set of owners is effectively eliminated. This reduces the ability of the owner to oversee public managers. Any benefit from improved efficiency is spread equally across all owners (those who monitor and those who do not), while the cost of monitoring is borne by the individual.

In summary, the property rights theorists point to differences in property rights—particularly the right to sell ownership shares—as the primary difference between public and private organizations. The owner of the private organization has virtually unrestricted right to sell or transfer ownership. The transferability of organization ownership, combined with the owner's right to the profit and capital value of the organization, gives the owner an incentive to oversee the organization's operations and maximize the technical efficiency of the organization. The owner of the public organization cannot sell or transfer ownership shares. Consequently, the incentives and advantages provided by transferability are lost. The owner and manager have less incentive to oversee organizational operations, less incentive to maximize the organization's present and future performance, and less incentive to maximize technical efficiency and minimize shirking.

Empirical Tests of Property Rights Theory. Most of the work in the property rights tradition has been theoretical. However, several empirical comparisons of public and private organizations have been undertaken in such service domains as electrical utilities (Neuberg, 1977; Di Lorenzo and Robinson, 1982), hospitals (Lindsay, 1976), water utilities (Bruggink, 1982), and airlines (Davies, 1977). Most have been limited to comparisons of technical efficiency, and most have supported the technical efficiency and property rights hypotheses.

A few of the studies falling within the property rights tradition have gone beyond simple comparison of technical efficiency. Davies (1981) suggests that the property rights argument implies that public managers will be more risk averse. The public manager cannot reap the benefits of long-term increase in the net worth of the organizations. Instead, "by avoiding errors of commission in contrast to errors of omission, the manager avoids a visible 'disaster' and the personal tragedy of transfer, demotion, or outright dismissal and assumes for himself a longer tenure in office and, consequently, a higher lifetime income" (Davies, 1981, p. 115). Davies found that the manager in a public bank tended to invest in less risky financial instruments. While there are few such comparisons to serve as a check against Davies' findings, it is worth noting that the many studies comparing risk-taking behavior in manager-controlled versus owner-controlled firms have yielded conflicting results (Bellante and Link, 1981; Capon, 1981).

Perhaps the most comprehensive empirical examination of organization behavior from a property rights perspective is Clarkson's (1972) analysis of public and private hospitals. He begins with Alchian's (1959) basic argument that limits on owner property rights in public organizations weaken controls over the manager and reduce the cost borne by the manager for nonproductive activities. The owners, or the owners' representatives, recognizing the difficulties of controlling the public manager, try to assert control by establishing explicit, formalized rules, regulations, and procedures. According to Clarkson (1972, p. 365), "nonproprietary hospitals will establish different sets of rules for the managers and employees; more specific bylaws and organizational purposes . . . ; staff meetings will be scheduled more often; formal budgets and accounts will be observed more often; criteria for success will be more difficult to discern; and allocative decisions within the firm will more often further 'nonproprietary' objectives."

Formal controls, however, are a poor substitute for automatic controls of the market. According to Clarkson, the manager of the nonproprietary organization will tend to deemphasize unpleasant tasks (such as monitoring and supervising subordinates) and emphasize pleasant activities—even when shirking the unpleasant tasks has a negative effect on productivity. Finally, Clarkson argues that rules, monitoring procedures, and factor inputs vary more across nonproprietary organizations because there is no incentive pushing toward the most efficient production technique.

Clarkson's hypotheses, on the whole, were strongly supported. He found that less time was spent on supervision by managers in nonproprietary hospitals and that proprietary hospitals were less likely to use formal budgets approved by the governing body and had fewer written regulations and fewer regular staff meetings. Wages among various job categories varied more in nonproprietary hospitals, as did several measures of cost efficiency.

Property Rights Theory: A Capsule Evaluation. One major limitation of property rights research is that few studies go beyond simple comparisons of cost or technical efficiency. By concentrating on narrow technical efficiency, using the same simple measures for both public and private organizations, property rights studies ignore the possibility that the goals and output of public and private organizations are incommensurable. For example, when Davies (1971, 1977) compares the efficiency of public and private airlines in Australia using such measures as passengers per employee, freight per employee, and revenue per employee, he implies that these criteria are equally valid and important across the two sectors. In reality, the public airline may have a variety of goals beyond these proprietary goals. It may desire to serve outlying communities, further the employment opportunities of minorities, or subsidize tourism. As public goods theory recognizes, activities are often allocated to the public sector because important externalities are recognized or because a good or service that cannot "turn a profit" nonetheless produces significant social value. In the public sector, cost effectiveness goals are balanced against such concerns as employment equity, representativeness, and distributional equity. Thus, comparison based only on technical efficiency and market-based criteria is limited at best.

Perhaps the most important limitation of property rights research is that the theory is almost never submitted to a valid test. Instead, theory is presented, differences in organizations are determined, and those differences are alleged to have resulted from effects specified in the theory. There is rarely much concern with rival hypotheses, and there is little reluctance to make bold inferential leaps. A finding that the cost of private provision of refuse collection is cheaper than public provision does not explain why the cost is lower. The tests of property rights theory have simply asserted that the causal stream leading to lower technical efficiency begins with property rights differences. There are a few studies (for example, Clarkson, 1972; Frech, 1980) that go so far as to examine the links between organization behavior and technical efficiency (rather than simply treating the organization as, for all intents and purposes, a blackbox). But none of the studies reviewed here does more than simply assert that these differences are caused by differences in the level of managerial concern for proprietary interests. These, in turn, are governed by a link between owner and managerial interests which is the product of property rights granted to the owners. The linkages are left untested.

The failure to fully test the theory is important because there is some question as to whether the hypothesized linkages exist, at least in the form assumed in property rights theory. As early as the 1930s, Berle and Means (1932) argued that ownership and control have been effectively separated in the modern corporate form of organization. Professional managers, they argued, make the decisions that establish organizational goals and operations. Galbraith (1967) has argued that stockholders exert no more control on the corporation than taxpayers do on the government organization. Studies (see reviews provided by De Alessi, 1980; James and Soref, 1981) seeking to empirically determine the impact of stockholders in comparison to the impact of owners in owner-managed firms have not come to consistent findings.

Another important problem with property rights theory, a problem especially relevant to present purposes, is a tendency to focus on stereotypical public organizations. As noted throughout this book, the world of organizations is not divided into a twofold classification table. Government-sponsored enterprises, multi-organization forms, public corporations, and other such organizational hybrids defy simple classification.

A Theory of "Privateness"? Despite the important limitations of property rights theory and research, there are several reasons why it deserves the attention of organization theorists (Moe, 1984). In particular, it provides the most detailed and best integrated explanation available as to the reasons why public and private organizations diverge.

Property rights theory is useful in the context of this book because it is plausible to assume (even if property rights theorists do not) that the economic authority associated with property rights is a matter of degree and, relatedly, that a wide variety of organizations, including public administrations, can possess property rights or their equivalent. Agencies charging user fees, government-sponsored enterprises, and nonprofit contractors all can be said to be imbued, to a degree, with elements of property rights. Just as publicness has pervasive effects on business, "privateness" (conveniently measured by constructs derived from property rights theory) has pervasive effects on government and other nonprofit organizations.

5

Political Authority:
Understanding the Roots
of Publicness

"Submission to order is almost always determined by a variety of motives," Weber (1947, p. 132) tells us. Sometimes "submission," including compliance with organizational directives, is best explained by the influence of economic authority. The organization provides economic inducements for persons inside and outside the organization. While there is some dispute (as demonstrated in the previous chapter) about the particular mechanisms of economic authority and their workings, it is easy to understand economic self-interest as a basis for action. Political compliance is not as easily understood. Do citizens, including organization members and clients, comply with political authority out of a sense of fear? Is it a "rational" response to the quality of service (Merelman, 1966) or to the coercive power of the state (Rothschild, 1977)? Is it respect for the state and its laws and recognition of the consequences of lawlessness (Friedrich, 1963)? Or is it a deep-seated sense of loyalty to shared traditions, political community, and political habits (Cochran, 1977)? And what of the motivational power of political symbols (Edelman, 1964)?

Property rights theory provides a useful and well-developed interpretation of the impact of economic authority on organization behavior. There is no comparable theoretical framework for explaining the impact of political authority on organizations, but instead a potpourri of assumptions and "grand theories," most of which do not directly address organization behavior.

Some of the leading controversies in the study of political authority are briefly reviewed below, but most of this chapter is devoted to developing a model of political authority directly applicable to the study of organization behavior. The model presented here is termed the *triadic model of political authority*, because it describes three types of political authority differentiated by the respective authority source from which each type flows. A central thesis of this book is that a theory of public organizations, as distinct from a theory of government organizations, should be based on a publicness concept that considers the dimensional character of publicness, can cope with sector blurring, and, in principle, is applicable to any modern complex organization. A concept of publicness as the level of political authority emanating from and constraining the organization meets these requirements.

Legitimacy and Political Authority

Political theorists writing about the nature of political authority have given little attention to the impact of political authority on organization behavior. Nevertheless, it is valuable to briefly review some of the leading controversies concerning legitimacy and political authority in order to place in context the organizationally relevant (but otherwise less ambitious) triadic model of political authority. Some of the questions that have drawn the attention of political theorists are pertinent to organization behavior, even if the theorists themselves have not drawn the connection. For example, political theorists have given much consideration to the question of political coercion, a topic closely related to organizational dependence and constraint. Likewise, questions about legitimacy are relevant to organizations' interactions with the public and relate to the public interest concerns of organizations.

Concepts of Legitimacy. It is often argued (see Schaar, 1970; Dahl, 1956; Runciman, 1963) that the political authority of the state is unique and that its uniqueness can be traced to the legitimacy of actions taken on behalf of the state. By some conceptions (Mainzer, 1973; Lowi, 1969), the cornerstone of political authority is the state's monopoly on the legitimate use of coercion. Legitimate political authority is distinct because it takes precedence over all other authority types and over the claims of any individual or group. But one can make the case that legitimacy is chiefly psychological (Edelman, 1964), that it is embodied in the individual, and that it exists "only when someone obeys out of a belief that he ought to do so" (Lindblom, 1977, p. 19).

One does not expect consensus on the meaning and implications of the fundamental abstractions of political theory. Thus it is not surprising to find that so elemental a concept as legitimacy has taken on many meanings and is used to serve many philosophical and instrumental purposes. Nor is it surprising that there is little agreement about how to (and even whether to) measure legitimacy (see, for example, Fraser, 1974). Yet despite the disagreement surrounding the concept, the issues upon which it turns are identifiable. One such issue is the relation of legitimacy to consent.

To Carl Friedrich (1963, p. 234), not only is consent a prerequisite of legitimacy, but it is a matter of whether "a given rulership is believed to be based on good title by most men subject to it." While such democratically oriented concepts of legitimacy are often well received, it is not clear whether they provide a firm foundation for government action. If legitimacy is dependent on individuals' contemporaneous assessments of the justness of government, legitimacy is necessarily volatile. If legitimacy is based on "good title," an explanation of the qualities of title must be supplied so that an assessment of its goodness can be made. Friedrich's concept of legitimacy is essentially Lockean and exhibits much the same problem as Locke's view of social contract. How are differences in individuals' perceptions of legitimacy resolved?

Critics of consent theory (such as McWilliams, 1971) have argued against its premises, especially against the notion that consent can be inferred. Consent cannot be inferred from receipt of state-provided benefits, because many benefits are collective goods and citizens cannot "avoid" benefit. Such political system supports as voting cannot be construed as consent unless the vote is a referendum on the state itself and not simply a choice among those who shall govern. Assuming that consent must be voluntary, one must be asked for his or her consent, there must be an opportunity for unfettered affirmation (or nonaffirmation) of that consent, and consent must be communicated. Further, consent cannot be a matter of disposition or attitude but must be expressed directly. These conditions are not easily met.

Even if it were possible to meet stringent conditions for the giving of consent, the problem of intersubjective differences in perception of obligation remains. One approach to resolving this problem is to define the individual's granting of consent in terms of social compact or obligations to one's fellow citizens rather than in terms of obligation to the state (Rawls, 1971). However, as Tussman (1960) notes, there are problems with assuming that a social contract agreed upon by one generation binds the next.

Some critics (such as Grafstein, 1981) charge that the chief flaw in most concepts of legitimacy, and especially in consent theory, is a focus on imputed but unknowable psychological states. It is argued that viewing legitimacy as a property of institutions is an effective means of avoiding mentalism (Martin, 1975). For legal positivist Hans Kelsen (1949), legitimacy is a matter of the validity of the laws of the state and conformance to authorized legal process. Peter Stillman (1974) takes this view a bit further and defines legitimacy in terms of the compatibility of government actions and the value patterns of the political system. Thus, legitimacy is not so volatile as public opinion, but neither is it fixed to a Hobbesian view of virtually unlimited state prerogatives.

Most legal positivist conceptions offer some analytical convenience in that they dismiss the psychological components of legitimacy and thus skirt one of the more formidable problems of theory. However, theories that fail to come to grips with the ritualistic and symbolic elements of political authority are open to charges of unrealism (Bennett, 1975; Cobb and Elder, 1973).

Some view the contradictions of theories of legitimacy as indicative of the dialectical nature of legitimacy. Kann (1978, p. 388) resolves the paradoxes of consent theories of legitimacy in terms of the dialectic by which "the government promotes conscientiousness and reason simultaneously [and] maximizes the potential for citizens to legitimate government." Kann feels that this dialectic is one that "promotes and tolerates the greatest challenge to its own authority." Morgan (1981) outlines a Madisonian view of political authority entailing a somewhat different dialectic pitting self-interest against stable institutions.

Legitimacy and Public Organization Theory. While most works on political legitimacy are concerned with the legitimacy of the state as a whole, questions of legitimacy are important to public organization theory in at least two ways. First, one must consider the character of the state as a pervasive environmental influence on the behavior of particular organizations (Frankel, 1972; Martin, 1975). Second, it is meaningful to speak of the legitimacy of particular organizations quite apart from the legitimacy of the state (Hannigan and Kueneman, 1977; Merelman, 1966).

A government organization created by statute is imbued with the political authority of the state and, as a result, the organization's legitimacy is linked to that of the state. For many business organizations, the question of political legitimacy is relatively unimportant. Many businesses are private agents acting independently on the basis of economic authority and the question of political legitimacy is only indirectly important insofar as it influences the legal environment of enterprise. But for many private nonprofit organizations and some businesses, the question of legitimacy is of more than passing interest. Many such organizations are endowed with political authority and thus are influenced directly by perceptions of the legitimacy not only of the state but also of the organization. For example, the American Bar Association is responsible for providing *pro bono publico* (for the public welfare) services for lawyers and for promulgating regulations that affect directly the conduct of the government system of justice. Likewise, boards of physicians are charged with similar public responsibilities for public health.

The countless advisory panels of government represent another case of private citizens and private organizations acting in a public capacity. For example, the National Science Board, a group of private individuals, is charged with significant policy-making responsibilities in science and technology. Perceptions of the legitimacy of such organizations can directly affect their ability to carry out effectively their public functions. The classic questions of legitimacy thus are pertinent to the political authority exercised by private as well as government organizations. Is the legitimacy of a physicians' review board largely a matter of legal designation, and thus is its public responsibility legally prescribed? Or is its public responsibility a matter of "good title"? If legitimacy is a matter of tolerating challenge to authority, then what does this say about the role of professionalism and technical expertise in the public arena?

While many of the classic questions of political theory are relevant to a theory of public organization behavior, it is not possible to simply direct the broader "answers" of political theory to the narrower "questions" of organization behavior. This is because political theory has been more valuable in raising the right questions about political authority than in providing answers. Many of the most basic questions of political authority remain unresolved. For example, none of the traditional rationales for legitimate political coercion is fully satisfying. Consent theory has moral appeal but is not easily translated into behavioral terms. Nor does consent theory resolve the problem of subjectivity. That is, if political authority ultimately resides with the individual, then it remains volatile. Social compact theory does not provide an adequate resolution because it is, at best, a complex mixture of consent, tradition, and habit. Legal positivism is not fully satisfying because it requires a level of agreement on procedure that is not easily guaranteed. Arguments about the supremacy of institutions in defining political legitimacy have the advantage of moving the focus away from mental states and disposition, but, in the process, they deny a role for the individual outside the framework of the institutions and thus leave one with a strong shell empty of content (Grady, 1976).

Thus, political theory, unlike property rights theory, does not provide an organizing framework for interpreting the effects of authority on organization behavior but does offer a useful point of departure. If there is any single lesson to be drawn from the diverse arguments about legitimacy and rationalization of political authority, it is that political authority is not best viewed as a unitary concept. In the discussion below, it is assumed that there are diverse sources and types of political authority, each with different implications for publicness and the behavior of organizations.

Three Types of Political Authority Endowments

Political authority can be characteized in many ways, but it is particularly useful to examine the source from which it flows and the endowments (rights, prerogatives) that result. Arguably, all political authority flows ultimately from individual citizens, but even if one takes that view it is still possible to speak of authority as mediated by institutions (Lipset, 1963). The triadic model of political authority addresses three different types of political authority. Before articulating the model, it is useful to describe each type of authority.

Primary political authority flows directly from individual citizens and is the bedrock of any political system. The ability of governments to make binding decisions is ultimately rooted in individuals' grants of legitimacy and in the commitments of individuals to both institutions and policies (Holmes, 1976). Despite the difficulties inherent in any attempt to measure or even map the flow of primary political authority, concepts of political authority based solely on institutional guarantors (see Kelsen, 1949; Stillman, 1974) are obviously incomplete. Institutions are created by individuals, commitments are made by individuals, and compliance to authority is an individual act.

As political theorists have noted, the subjectivity of individuals' judgments about the legitimacy of political acts adds an ingredient of volatility to public affairs, but one that is unavoidable and, in many respects, desirable. Historical analyses of revolution (Arendt, 1963) have demonstrated that individuals' grants of legitimacy are not immutable. Further, mass resistance to public policy (such as draft resistance during the Vietnam War and tax protest movements) is a reminder that individual grants of legitimacy are volatile.

Whereas primary political authority connects with consent theory, *secondary political authority* finds its counterparts in institutionally oriented and legal positivist theories of legitimacy. The necessity of delegating grants of authority to the polity is as much a matter of practical utility as of political philosophy. The size of the modern nation-state dictates that direct democracy is not viable for most policy initiatives and certainly not for the routine functioning of government. Secondary political authority is exercised by public officials, both elected and nonelected (including government bureaucrats and civil servants), charged with acting on behalf of the citizenry.

The grant of secondary authority is not without form and substance. In the United States, secondary authority obviously is constrained by the Constitution and accumulated statutes. But secondary political authority is not exclusively grounded in formal public policies. Indeed, it is a mistake even to define secondary authority exclusively in terms of policy. There is another element that is vitally important to an organizationally relevant concept of publicness: The term *governance structure* is used here to refer to the relatively stable patterns of political process that shape the conduct of public affairs in both the public and the private sector. The point is elaborated in a subsequent section.

Whereas primary political authority is vested in the individual citizen and secondary political authority in official institutions of government, *tertiary political authority* pertains to nongovernment organizations and private citizens. Tertiary political authority is delegated authority twice removed. Public officials are viewed as the delegates of private citizens, and these delegates sometimes endow private organizations (including business, nonprofit, and "mixed form" organizations) with political authority to act on behalf of the public. The vesting of political authority in private organizations differs from the much more common vesting of economic interests (Roy, 1981). In the latter case, the agency actively (but indirectly) represents the interest of private groups and organizations; in the former case, the private party is actually endowed with formal political authority, which is exercised directly.

Thus, some private organizations are, at the same time, constrained by secondary political authority (via government regulations, statutes, and so forth) and endowed with tertiary authority. This is a situation not unlike that in which most government organizations find themselves—endowed with secondary authority but, at the same time, subject to its constraints as dictated by government superiors. This parallel is useful in facilitating a theory of publicness based not on the legal status of organizations but on the effects of political authority. The relationship between political constraints and endowments is discussed in Chapter Six.

Political Authority and Organization Behavior

Each of the three types of political authority enumerated above has implications for the behavior of individual organizations. Even primary political authority, which seems far removed from the day-to-day business of organizations, can be an important determinant of organizational actions and outcomes. Subsequently, the triadic model of political authority provides a description of the impact of political authority on organization behavior. First, however, it is useful to consider in turn how each type of political authority influences organization behavior.

Primary Political Authority and Organization Behavior

In the United States, citizens' views of the legitimacy of the state tend to be stable. Where there are major shifts in the citizenry's perceptions of the legitimacy of the state, the implications are enormous not only for organization behavior but also for general social upheaval. In such cases, organizations are affected for much the same reasons as are other social institutions, and thus these effects are not of special interest to organization behavior (but are more within the realm of social theory). But primary political authority affects organization behavior in a variety of ways, not just as a result of system changes in the legitimacy of the state.

It is convenient to view primary political authority as having effects at different orders of magnitude or at different "levels" of influence. At the most general level, primary political authority affects organization behavior as a result of shifts in the citizenry's assessments of the legitimacy of the state. At the most specific level, individual citizens' assessments of specific policies represent an influence of primary political authority.

Level I Influence: Assessments of the Legitimacy of the State. Individual grants of legitimacy are selective, and thus the effects of primary political authority are only rarely direct. Obviously, one does not consciously consider each public policy issue that arises and evaluate it in terms of one's commitment to the legitimacy of the state. On most occasions, Level I primary political authority is on "automatic pilot." Individuals are only episodically motivated to reevaluate grants of legitimacy (Kourvetaris and Dobratz, 1982). The political system of the United States has been sufficiently stable that the only conspicuous and clear-cut example of Level I influence during the last 200 years is the Civil War. The secessionists, whether motivated by economic self-interest in slavery, loyalty to tradition and region, or whatever, were by the act of secession declaring void the sovereignty of the United States government.

It is axiomatic that large-scale challenges to legitimacy are of sweeping consequence. But despite the United States experience, it is not the case that Level I political authority influence is either exceedingly rare or necessarily violent. As a case in point, consider the Mexican political system. In Mexico, massive changes in political systems have been frequent and, at least in some instances, nonviolent (Padgett, 1966). Of course, not every coup, whether violent or nonviolent, represents an influence of Level I political authority. Government changes based on personal power struggles are not often political system changes.

Level II Influence: Assessments of the Role and Scope of Government. Somewhat more common than shifts in views of the legitimacy of government are shifts in assessments of the appropriate scope and role of state activity. Level II changes are illustrated by Franklin Roosevelt's New Deal and, perhaps, by the Reagan presidency. It is an oversimplification to say that the New Deal and the Reagan presidency can be explained entirely in terms of shifts in the citizenry's assessment of the scope and role of state activity. Public responses sometimes are better explained by perceptions of the president's personal effectiveness than by ideology (Hibbs, 1982). Furthermore, proactive presidents forge their own agendas and, of course, a variety of policy-making institutions shape policy. The Taft Supreme Court and the Tip O'Neill–led House of Representatives show that policy-making institutions are often in fundamental disagreement about the appropriate scope and role of government. Nonetheless, presidential elections are the closest the United States comes to a national referendum, and there is perhaps no better bellwether of shifts in citizens' assessments of the role of the state.

The effects of Level II changes are enormous. Events such as the New Deal have far-reaching effects on the populations of organizations and on the ecology of whole classes of organizations. Kaufman (1976) has noted that federal government agencies' patterns of birth and decline are best accounted for by shifts in epochs. Similarly, students of organization life cycles (Kimberly, Miles, and Associates, 1980; Kaufman, 1985) draw attention to the changes arising from such systemic effects. Primary political authority affects organization behavior through its role in determining the state's sphere of activity. In this manner, primary political authority affects not only the rise and demise of federal agencies but also the fates of business organizations. For example, the Reagan administration's emphasis on "privatization" not only has curtailed the programs and activities of federal agencies but also has shifted policy direction toward state and municipal governments (Palmer and Sawhill, 1982) and affected the range and type of activities performed by business organizations (Levine, 1986).

Levels III and IV Influence: Assessments of Policies. In some instances, public opinion is focused on general classes of policy actions—"macropolicies"; at other times, it is focused on specific policies—"micropolicies." For example, the public's views about national security and defense are often expressed in broad, unfocused terms (for example, "too much money is spent on defense"; "there is a weapons gap"). Less commonly, public opinion sometimes centers on a specific policy action (such as aid to the contras in Nicaragua). In each case, primary political authority plays a role in shaping organization behavior. A major shift in assessments of macropolicies is, for present purposes, an instance of Level III influence and, similarly, the arousal of public opinion in connection with micropolicies is an instance of Level IV influence. Note that the use of the terms *shift* and *arousal* denotes an important distinction. The macropolicies of Level III are sufficiently broad that there is a presumption of long-standing, if changeable, public opinion. Level III macropolicies are enduring. By contrast, a long-term public opinion cannot be presumed for micropolicies of Level IV, not only because the issues are more specific but also because they are shorter term.

In many cases, the effects of Level III and IV exercises in primary political authority directly affect government organizations and indirectly affect other organizations. If the conviction that there should be an expanded defense establishment is acted on, the the agencies of the Department of Defense (and "losers" in other budget categories) are directly affected, but the indirect effects for other organizations are substantial, especially in regions of the country where defense contractors and organizations are economically significant.

In sum, primary political authority is exercised in several ways, and for each level of activity there are strong implications for government and nongovernment organizations. Primary political authority, regardless of level, is unique in that it originates with individual citizens and their perceptions of the political environment. These perceptions are not colored by such institutions as the media, government, and political parties. Likewise, organizations and social institutions play a critical role in translating and channeling primary political authority (Hess, 1963) and in political participation. This means that it is quite difficult to trace the effects of primary political authority because it is so intertwined with other policy influences (such as elections, secondary political authority, interest group activity, and lobbying) and with perceptions of individual political actors and their roles (Weissberg, 1972; Greenstein, 1960). Nonetheless, primary political authority is as important as it is difficult to fathom.

Secondary Political Authority and Organization Behavior

When one reflects on the impact of publicness on the behavior of organizations, the examples that first come to mind are those involving the exercise of secondary political authority. Organizations are affected by statutes, administrative rules and regulations, executive orders, and judicial mandates. In many instances, these impacts are direct and easily understood: The courts break up American Telephone and Telegraph (AT&T), the Occupational Safety and Health Administration (OSHA) closes down a construction project because of unsafe working conditions, a state legislature passes an excise tax on alcoholic beverages—each of these constraints is easily understood as an instance of the effects of publicness on the behavior of organizations. Likewise, each might be viewed as yet another instance of "government climbing on the back of industry." Or, to put it another way, secondary political authority affects not just government organizations but others as well.

To recapitulate, the source of secondary political authority is, by definition, public officials working within the framework of formally designated government institutions. As is the case for primary political authority, the source of authority is invariate, but the type of output or influence is not. While there are a great many ways to classify the outputs of government bodies, for purposes of understanding the effects of political authority a distinction must be made among *policy constraints and benefits, endowments,* and *governance structures.* Roughly, these influences on organization behavior can be thought of, respectively, as public policy outputs, delegations of political authority, and structural features of policy processes. Moreover, the exercise of secondary political authority may result in influence of each type. Consider as an example the award of a defense contract. It is an endowment because, by definition, it permits the private contractor to perform activity on behalf of the government. It thereby extends the authority of the private contractor. It is a constraint in that the contract specifies obligations of the contractor and imposes performance requirements. The issue of governance structures is less clear-cut.

Governance structures are defined as the relatively stable patterns of political process that shape the conduct of public affairs. To put it simply, the effects of publicness on organization behavior accrue as often from policy process as from policy substance. To extend the example of the defense contractor, the behavior of the focal organization (the contractor) is affected not only by the specific constraints and grants of authority embodied in the DOD-contractor relationship but also by the processes that inevitably follow from interaction with a public policy agent such as the Department of Defense. In addition to any specific requirements set by the contract, the contractor is inexorably affected by government accounting and purchasing procedures, affirmative action and Equal Employment Opportunity (EEO) hiring requirements, freedom of information provisions, and other such routine features of public processes. Since governance structures are vitally important to the understanding of the impact of political authority on organizations, some elaboration of the concept is required.

Governance Structures: The Publicness of Process. A focus on governance structures is especially appropriate in any attempt to build public organization theory. Whereas the grants of authority and the constraints flowing from secondary political authority are highly idiosyncratic and sometimes difficult to classify, policy process effects are more stable, more easily classified, and more predictable. It is useful to distinguish between two types of governance structures. Popular discussions of the "strings" attached by government involvement often pertain to governance structures. We shall refer to these "strings" as *policy routines*. In addition to policy routines, there is another category of governance structures that is more fundamental and more stable: Governance structures such as the federal system, separation of powers, and other such rudimentary structures are referred to as *policy system elements*. Policy routines and policy system elements are often closely related such that many policy routines are shaped by policy system elements. For example, the minute specifications for General Accounting Office (GAO) audits can be understood, at least in part, as manifestations of the constitutional principle of separation of powers. Indeed, the U.S. Constitution is perhaps the most important determinant of the effects of process on organization behavior.

Policy System Elements and the Constitution. Peter Woll (1977, p. 64) aptly describes the influence of the U.S. Constitution on public bureaucracy: "The effect of the Constitution is to fragment the bureaucracy. Lines of control are blurred, organization patterns are diverse, and in general unity is absent. The Constitution has fragmented our political system generally and the bureaucracy is not an exception." Woll's interpretation of the impact of the Constitution on public bureaucracy is well taken but, if anything, it is too limiting. The Constitution touches not only public bureaucracies but organizations of all types. Not only does it directly constrain the range of permissible political action, but it also serves as a powerful political symbol (Baas, 1979). By shaping governance structures in general and by setting policy system elements in particular, the Constitution establishes the framework for policy and for the impact of publicness on organizations.

There are several ways in which the Constitution fragments government in general. As an illustration, let us consider the constitutional principle of separation of powers. The effects are especially pronounced in the case of government agencies. Agencies are directed by executive superiors, dependent on legislators for resources, and subject to the rules, interpretations, and injunctions of the judicial branch. When one further considers the constraints imposed by agencies of the public bureaucracy, which have central authority on such matters as fiscal and budgetary policy (for example, the Office of Management and Budget), procurement and facilities management (the General Services Administration), and personnel procedures and policies (the Office of Personnel Management), it becomes clear that the government agency serves many masters.

While the fragmentation embodied in the Constitution is one of the more important means by which the behavior of public agencies is shaped, there are other important respects in which the Constitution influences government organizations. According to

Wilson (1975), developments as diverse as the rise of clientism in regulatory agencies and bureaucratic inertia can be understood in terms of constitutional factors.

Typically, the nongovernment organization is less subject to diverse external authorities. Nevertheless, the policy system elements created under the Constitution and the policy routines reflecting such elements as separation of powers can affect the behaviors of nongovernment organizations. Consider the case of a giant corporation which includes among its many activities production of weapons systems for the Department of Defense. In many of its activities, at least those that are proprietary and that proceed on the basis of market demand, the corporation will maintain a high degree of autonomy in setting and pursuing its goals, in managing its resources, and in determining its personnel procedures. However, the DOD contract brings with it the imprint of the federal government's governance structures. The intragovernmental fragmentation resulting from the constitutional principle of separation of powers has direct and immediate effects on the corporation. At least in regard to the activities under the DOD contract, the corporation now is accountable not only to DOD contract officers but perhaps also to GAO auditors, General Services Administration (GSA) purchasing policies, and Office of Management and Budget (OMB) regulations about contracts and reporting procedures. Further, the corporation now may become an object of attention of congressional watchdogs and may be called upon to testify at congressional and executive budget proceedings. The intragovernmental fragmentation of the federal government fragments the authority of the corporation.

Governance Structures and Policy Routines. Some policy routines can be viewed as direct outgrowths of policy system elements. For example, the intragovernmental fragmentation that arises from the constitutional principle of federalism shapes policy routines pertaining to tax collection and, in turn, affects the behaviors of all tax-paying organizations. Other policy routines have developed more or less independently. Sharkansky (1970, p. 29) defines routines as "procedures, habits, and learned behaviors that are evident in the decision processes of individuals, social groups, and formal organizations." Usually routines emerge as simplifying or stabilizing devices, but once institutionalized, they take on a momentum that goes beyond any initial rationale (Tolbert and Zucker, 1983).

As an example of the impact of routines on organization behavior, consider the many routines of the federal budgetary process. Whereas organizations operating entirely on the basis of economic authority are free to expend resources at any desired rate, acquire resources from any source, and develop their own accounting and budgeting protocols, organizations subject to federal budgeting routines are affected by such factors as budget cycles, the annual nature of most appropriations processes, the separation of authorization and appropriations, and the incremental nature of budgeting. These routines affect not only government agencies but also business organizations dependent on government appropriations, subsidy, and contracts. Consider the case of private research universities heavily dependent on state government appropriations and federal grants. Relevant policy routines influence the universities' budgeting and accounting policies, resource management strategies, and planning procedures. A strong flavor of publicness is brought to any organization tied to the policy routines of government budgeting.

Tertiary Political Authority and Organization Behavior

Tertiary political authority is similar to the grants of authority provided by secondary political authority. But whereas secondary political authority permits the focal organization to engage in certain specified activities (for example, building a new jet fighter, using a NASA satellite to transmit signals, receiving a tax credit for expenditures on research and development), tertiary authority vests policy-making power in the organization. Thus, it is a grant of authority of a peculiar type. With tertiary political authority, the organization becomes a policy actor. The effects of tertiary political authority are profound because the organization's behavior is not simply affected by publicness: Its behavior *is* public. Under this peculiar endowment of authority, the focal organization is empowered to exercise secondary authority.

In the vast majority of instances, tertiary political authority is restricted to government agencies. Since the granting of tertiary authority is, in most respects, equivalent to granting governmental status, it may seem trivial to suggest that tertiary authority is restricted to government agencies. But this seemingly obvious assumption of equivalency between tertiary political status and formal governmental legal status deserves closer inspection. In the first place, there are private entities that are granted authority to act with the full backing of government and with the force of law while at the same time preserving their private status. Only a few examples come to mind, most of which are professional organizations, such as physicians' review boards, American Bar Association licensing boards, and so forth. The more important—or at least more pervasive—instance of private organizations receiving grants of tertiary authority is multi-organization entities which include some subunits that retain purely private status and some that have governmental policy-making authority. A few fully private organizations (as opposed to quasi-private entities, such as the Tennessee Valley Authority) have been set up with the encouragement and through the initiative of government. An example is Comsat (Musolf, 1983), an organization set up as a legitimate monopoly in communications. Another instance of tertiary authority flowing to a private organizational actor is the government-owned, contractor-operated Department of Energy laboratories. While the political authority of the contract operator is limited to management of the government entity under its purview, this narrow policy-making responsibility is nonetheless an instance of tertiary political authority.

In addition to those cases in which legitimate political authority is formally delegated to private organizations, there is also a suggestion that most corporations are by their very nature minigovernments (Eells, 1962; Blumberg, 1971). Vogel (1975) argues that the development of the large corporation has devolved from its original and limited grant of legitimacy into public operations for which it has no formal grant of authority. Vogel observes that (1) citizens make demands directly to corporations, (2) citizens behave toward corporations in a way similar to the way in which they interact with the state, and (3) citizens apply a standard of accountability to corporations similar to that applied to government. When these facts are taken together with corporations' increasing concern with social forces, the corporation is best viewed as a public organization, Vogel argues.

Tertiary political authority is an interesting question in organization theory because of the rise of new organizational forms and the rethinking of allocations of political authority. However, tertiary political authority is still much more common to governmental agencies than to other organization forms, and an understanding of tertiary political authority requires examination of the processes by which government agencies are created by other government agencies.

A Triadic Model of Political Authority

The theory presented in this book seeks to provide an alternative view of publicness relevant to the explanation of organizations' behavior. Publicness is not viewed as an absolute quality but as a dimension. The dimension is defined by the organization's mix of economic and political authority as a basis of its activity. In Chapter Four, it is argued that conventional property rights theory provides an acceptable, although not ideal, explanation of the effects of economic authority on organization behavior. Property rights theory is, in some respects, tailor-made for a public organization theory. Such is not the case with political authority. The nature of political authority is not always clear, and there is little agreement as to the causal processes by which political authority affects organization behavior.

This chapter has presented a view in which three types of political authority flow from diverse sources, with both direct and indirect influences, and entailing a variety of impacts, alternately enhancing, constraining, and legitimizing the actions of the focal organization. The effects of political authority on organization behavior are not easy to determine or to conceptualize. Conceptual difficulty is explained by a number of factors. The most important is the complexity of effects. Complexity in this case arises from the breadth of impact, the simultaneous effects of diverse sources of political authority, and the difficulty in separating effects of

Figure 5.1. Triadic Model of the Effects of Political Authority
on Organization Behavior.

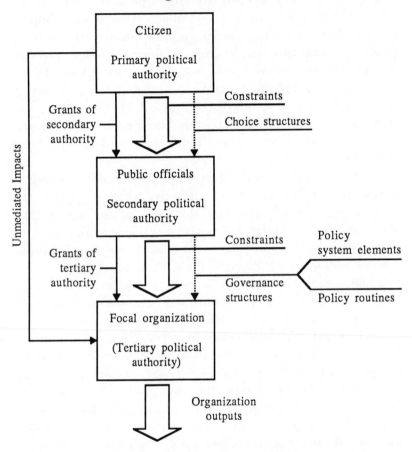

political authority (given their breadth) from other environmental
infuences, especially those that are economic in origin, on
organization behavior. Nevertheless, it is necessary to attempt some
depiction of the impacts of political authority on organization
behavior, and Figure 5.1 represents a beginning attempt to sort
through the complexity.

The triadic model assumes that it is useful to distinguish
among the effects of three distinct types of political authority. As
represented in Figure 5.1, the model suggests that: (1) individuals,
acting on endowments of primary authority, delegate decision

authority to public officials; (2) public officials formulate laws and shape governance structures that affect organizations; (3) the behavior of organizations, both governmental and nongovernmental, is affected by endowments and constraints arising from secondary authority and, at least in some instances, primary authority; (4) the behavior of organizations is also affected by the governance structures that determine the channels for distribution of authority as well as acceptable protocol for compliance; and (5) for some organizations, tertiary authority confers on organizations the ability to perform as a public actor with governmental legitimacy.

The triadic model is highly simplified and does not seek to account for the determinants of authority; nor does it specify the range or quality of values for the terms of the model. The objectives of this abbreviated model are (1) to distinguish three types of political authority, (2) to demonstrate the flow of various types of political authority, and (3) to show in a highly general way that organization behavior is influenced by grants of tertiary political authority, constraints of primary and secondary political authority, and the channeling effects of governance structures.

In considering the triadic model in connection with the dimensional theory of publicness developed in the next chapter, two points are worth noting. First, the triadic model suggests that the influence of political authority is independent of sector. While one might well expect that government organizations typically would be subject to a wider range of political authority influences than would private organizations and that those influences might be stronger relative to other environmental influences, the model is just as applicable to business, third-sector, government enterprise, and mixed form organizations as it is to traditional government agencies. Property rights theory is a model of economic authority that is applicable to any organizational form, and for purposes of symmetry it is necessary that the model of political authority developed here is likewise applicable to any organization form.

A second point is perhaps implicit in the model. As the dimensional theory is developed in the next chapter, it is necessary to assume that the impacts of political and economic authority are

Figure 5.2. Effects of Political Authority on Economic Authority.

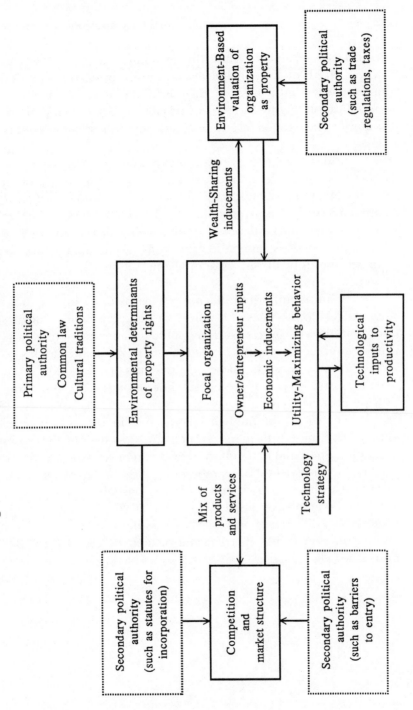

distinct and separable. While this assumption is suitable to the current state of knowledge about public organizations and environmental influences on their behavior, it is nonetheless a simplification. Figure 5.2, presented below, indicates that political authority and economic authority are interrelated in important ways.

At the deepest level, political and economic cornerstones of a society are built on common cultural ground. For this reason, if for no other, one would expect significant mutual influence between political and economic authority. When we further consider that much of public policy—perhaps the majority of domestic policy—is rationalized in terms of economic goals, we can see the difficulty of separating one social instrument from another.

Political authority influences the behavior of any organization subject to the rules of a polity. In some cases, those impacts are from distant sources (such as public opinion); in other cases those impacts are proximate and direct (for instance, audits of government contracts). In some cases, the impacts flow from characteristics of policy processes, while in others they flow from the policies themselves.

The theory of publicness presented in the next chapter argues that the key to the publicness puzzle is the organization's mix of political and economic authority. An organization is "more public" to the extent that its ratio of political authority increases. Political authority carries with it diverse constraints, prerogatives, and even symbols (Goodsell, 1977; Pool, 1952). The organization subject to political authority may, as a result, become more or less powerful, more or less effective, and/or more or less adaptive, but it is sure to be changed.

6

Why All Organizations Are Public: A Multi-Dimensional View of Publicness

Let us break the suspense: all organizations are public because political authority affects some of the behavior and processes of all organizations. This simple allegation contains in it the seeds of a theory of publicness. It implies that: (1) *public* pertains to the effects of political authority; (2) organizations can be more public in respect to some activities and less public in respect to others; (3) all organizations are public, but some are more public than others.

This chapter builds on the preceding two chapters and presents the elements and basic assumptions of a multi-dimensional view of publicness, a view that is applicable to the broad spectrum of modern organizations. Why multi-dimensional? Because publicness is not a discrete quality that is present in its whole or wholly absent. Nor does the organizational universe consist of only two worlds—the world of public organizations and the world of private organizations—with no interplanetary travel or communication. The multi-dimensional theory assumes that modern organizations, regardless of sector or type, are influenced by both political and economic authority and typically exert both types of authority.

The outline for a multi-dimensional view of publicness begins with a statement of three basic axioms and then moves to a discussion of the dynamics of the theory and finally to a discussion of the impact of publicness on the essential processes of organizations.

A Multi-Dimensional Theory: Three Axioms

The publicness concept presented here might be termed *public-as-authority mix*. An organization (any organization, regardless of sector or morphology) is public to the extent that it exercises or is constrained by political authority. An organization is private to the extent that it exercises or is constrained by economic authority. There are several implications of this and the other axiomatic assumptions presented below. Perhaps the most important implication, however, is that a multi-dimensional view of publicness provides a means of dealing with sector blurring and hybrid organizations and, at least in this respect, represents an improvement on the public-as-government concept.

The Multi-Dimensional Assumption

> Axiom 1: Publicness is not a discrete quality but a multi-dimensional property. An organization is public to the extent that it exerts or is constrained by political authority.

The multi-dimensional assumption is the cornerstone of the theory presented here. While such a concept of publicness is not without its problems (How is publicness measured? What are the behavioral consequences of various degrees of publicness?), it is nonetheless in accord with contemporary organizational realities: many "private" firms are heavily subsidized by government agencies, "public" organizations are increasingly dependent on the market, and many organizations are not easily classified as public or private.

The concern here is with public organization theory, but the discussion of publicness should not be taken as evidence of unconcern about privateness. In most instances, the term *public-ness* is used as a shorthand for the organization's location on a publicness-privateness dimension. Indeed, Corollary 1 makes explicit the importance of privateness:

> Corollary 1: An organization is private to the extent that it exerts or is constrained by economic authority.

Few, if any, complex organizations are purely public or purely private. Instead, there is some mix of public and private authority influencing the behavior of organizations. The key issue, then, is to determine the mix of authority for the organization and the impact of particular configurations of authority on organization behavior. Thus, Corollary 2 is crucial to the eventual development of empirical measures for the multi-dimensional theory:

> Corollary 2: Since organizations can be viewed as more or less public and, at the same time, more or less private (in terms of the influence of authority), any organization can be considered in terms of its authority mix. Authority mix is the proportions of economic and political authority influencing the organization.

If publicness is multi-dimensional rather than discrete, and if organization publicness-privateness can be viewed in terms of authority mix, it is apparent that the conventional equating of publicness (privateness) solely with formal legal status is inappropriate:

> Corollary 3: Publicness is independent of the formal legal status of the organization. Some government organizations are more public than others; some business organizations are more public than others; some business organizations are more public in some respects [see Axiom 2] than are some government organizations.

The Decomposition Assumption: Disaggregated Publicness

> Axiom 2: A given organization may be more influenced by political authority in some of its processes and behaviors than in others and thus can be said to be more public in some of its processes and behaviors and less so in others.

Using the multi-dimensional concept of publicness, it is possible to develop indicators of the degree of publicness/privateness of organizations. But such indicators are necessarily either aggregate or partial measures because, under the decomposition assumption, it is argued that any given organization may be more public in regard to some of its activities and less so in regard to others. That is, an organization may exercise more political authority in connection with, say, goal setting. Thus, the decomposition assumption holds that particular organizations are not wholly public or private but are more or less public in respect to particular aspects of organizational activity.

The decomposition assumption adds complexity to the organization theorist's taxonomic and measurement tasks, but that complexity is redeemed by an extra measure of realism in the depiction of organizations and their processes.

The Equivalency Assumption

> Axiom 3: For purposes of judging the impact of publicness on organization behavior, it can be assumed that political constraint is equivalent to political endowment. It is unnecessary to distinguish the motives underlying the influence of political authority.

An important assumption of the theory is that external imposition of political authority (that is, political constraints) and external endowment of political authority can, for purposes of the theory, be viewed as roughly equivalent. That is to say, the behavior of the organization is more public in both instances—

when it is constrained by political authority and when it is endowed with political authority. (The same is true, of course, in regard to economic authority.)

While it is unconventional, to say the least, to assume that constraint of authority and endowment of authority are equivalent, the assumption seems less remarkable when one considers the object of the theory. The purpose is not to describe organization influence, effectiveness, or strength; nor is the purpose to account for the full range of determinants of organizational behavior. Instead, the purpose is to understand the significance of publicness as an influence on organization behavior. From that more limited perspective, it matters little whether the organization is acting as a result of endowment or constraint. It is not the source of publicness (or privateness) that matters, but its impact. This assumption of the equivalency of internal and external authority has a number of advantages. It removes the necessity to identify the roles and gauge the purposes of particular actors.

Let us consider an example that illustrates the merits of the equivalency assumption. The state legislature passes a law requiring that all school boards require public school teachers to take competency exams every five years. Despite the protests of the teachers' unions and individual teachers, the head of the local school board implements the mandate. An understanding of the impact of publicness in this episode of organizational behavior does not require an accounting of the mental processes of the chairperson of the school board. Whether the chair of the school board enforced the mandate against his or her will or whether he or she viewed the mandate as an increment to the political authority of the board and gleefully seized the opportunity to enforce the mandate, the result is the same: The legitimate coercive power of the state is exercised and, along with it, so is all the attendant consequence of political authority (such as governance structures specifying appeals channels).

Dynamics of a Multi-Dimensional Theory of Publicness

The crux of the argument presented thus far is easily summarized: Political authority affects the behavior of organizations because certain legal, political, cultural, and psychological constraints invariably accompany the exercise of political authority. Even business organizations operating in the marketplace are inexorably affected by delegations of political authority or by compliance with political authority. Likewise, economic authority has pervasive effects. But both government and business organizations vary in the extent to which they exert economic authority and are influenced by economic authority exerted on them by external agents. A multi-dimensional theory interprets organization behavior in terms of the mix of economic and political authority of an organization.

The multi-dimensional theory of publicness is represented in Figure 6.1. The multi-dimensional theory appropriates the theoretical arguments of Chapters Four and Five concerning, respectively, the effects of economic and political authority on organization behavior. Implicit in the representation of the theory given in Figure 6.1 (and deducible from the defining assumption given above) is the melding of economic and political authority. A given external actor may exert some combination of economic and political authority and, likewise, the focal organization can exert some combination of economic and political authority on the external environment.

It is expected that the impact of economic authority will be somewhat more stable and predictable than the impact of political authority. This is because political authority is defined in terms of the particulars of primary political authority (usually indirect and difficult to map) and secondary authority (as stable or unstable as the policies promulgated by public officials). The more stable and predictable impacts of political authority are those flowing from governance structures.

Figure 6.1 shows impacts of authority on organizations but indicates that the effects are mediated by characteristics of the organization. This assumption gives rise to the hypotheses that follow.

Mediating Assumption: The Role of Buffers. Organizations are not uniform in their response to political authority. Obviously, political acts are sometimes tailored to particular organizations or

Figure 6.1. Multi-Dimensional Theory of the Impact of Publicness
on Organization Behavior.

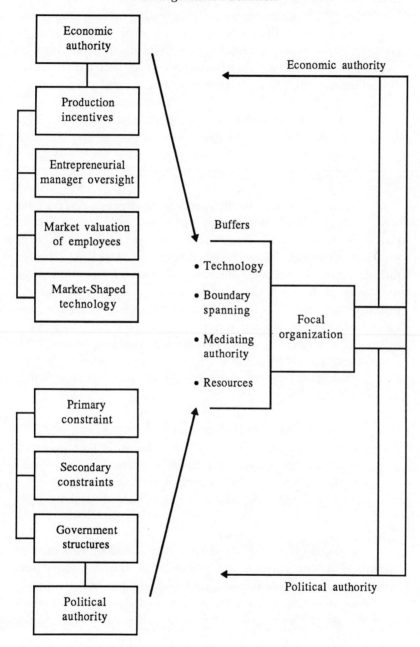

to individual organizations. But much of the variation in organizations' outcomes resulting from political acts relates to the "buffering" ability of organizations. Organizations devise numerous mechanisms for dealing with environmentally induced change. However, some of the mechanisms are particularly important with respect to environmental change resulting from political authority. One of the most important buffers is authority itself.

> Mediating Hypothesis 1: Organizations employ existing political authority endowments (mediating authority) to mediate the impact of new, externally imposed political authority.

While it may well be the case that the organization does not wish to resist (and indeed may cultivate) externally imposed political authority, it often has the option of using existing political authority endowments as a buffer. Used as a buffer, political authority becomes mediating authority. In some instances, mediating authority flows directly from the focal organization's political authority, which it can exercise through external actors. In other instances, mediating authority results from links to influential political allies. Thus, an organization mandated by a superior government agency to perform a given act might initiate an "end run" by using its influence with a legislator to either overturn or modify the mandate.

> Mediating Hypothesis 2: External imposition of political authority tends to have greater impact on organizations with a low basis of alternative (economic) authority. Organizations seek to substitute authority types in order to exert control over their environment.

Authority types are not directly substitutable. However, an organization with considerable economic wherewithal often finds itself in a different position in regard to external political authority than does an organization with little economic authority on which to trade. By the same token, an organization with considerable political authority often can use that authority to buffer economic changes. Thus, for example, a focal organization may use its political authority to persuade an ally to enjoin economic rivals from using allegedly noncompetitive practices.

> Mediating Hypothesis 3: The indigenous resources of the organization act to buffer external political authority.

Pervasive though it is, authority is not the only dimension along which organizations vary. Any of several indigenous resources can affect organizations' responses to externally imposed political authority (Provan, Beyer, and Kruybosch, 1980; Whetten and Bozeman, forthcoming). Some of these include: general competence and particular skills of management, level and flexibility of financial resources, composition of the labor force, reputation and general public perceptions, and supplies of natural resources and production inputs.

> Mediating Hypothesis 4: Organizational technology buffers the effects of external political authority.

The effects of political authority often are distributed according to organization technology and organization product type (Emery and Trist, 1965; Downs, 1967). Organizations have various means of sheltering their core technology (Thompson, 1967) from the environment, including interactions associated with external political authority.

> Mediating Hypothesis 5: Boundary-spanning activities mitigate the effects of external political authority.

Miles (1980, p. 316) observes that "organizations do not scan their environments, interpret what they see, and translate and communicate findings to their decision makers. . . . decision makers rely on *people* occupying special roles to perform these boundary-spanning and maintaining functions on behalf of their organizations." Since no organization exists in a vacuum, boundary-spanning activity is omnipresent. But organizations vary substantially in the level and formality of boundary-spanning activity (Aldrich, 1979; Aldrich and Herker, 1977). Boundary-spanning activities help determine the amount, timing, and quality of information about the environment and, perhaps more important, sometimes permit the organization to shape its enacted environment. Thus, boundary spanning is a critical contingency in the organization's ability to mediate the effects of external political authority. Sometimes this mediation aims at creating or exploiting opportunities (such as procuring appropriations or contracts, lobbying), and sometimes it aims at identifying and diminishing threats (potential budget cutbacks, downturns in the market).

Publicness and Constraint. The multi-dimensional theory is, in large measure, an interpretation of the impact of diverse constraints. But it is important to note that constraint takes on a special meaning here. In many uses, the term takes on a pejorative meaning. Constraint is often accompanied by such qualifying adjectives as "undue," "unnecessary," or "burdensome." Constraints are to be avoided. The usage here is not intended to carry such connotations. It is assumed that constraints can be viewed by the organization or the manager as positive, negative, or neutral in value. Consider, for example, the changing role of the Interstate Commerce Commission (ICC) in regulating the railroad industry (Woll, 1977). During the early history of the ICC, its regulations were viewed as limiting and railroad barons took a dim view of ICC constraints. Later, ICC regulations provided an economic shelter for railroads and constraints had a positive value for owners and investors. Both sets of regulatory policies—those limiting monopolistic practices as well as those sheltering the railroad from a transportation market in which it could no longer compete successfully—are constraints.

Given the focus on constraint as an important element of publicness, one might well question the value of examining political constraint instead of constraint in general. Why is political constraint special? Consider the case of two different constraints on a firm: (1) a mandate to implement a minority training program so as to enhance the recruitment and advancement of minority employees; (2) a cash grant to stimulate R & D activity. Consider the implications of each from the perspective of (a) a mandate from a parent company; (b) an internal directive from the CEO of the focal organization; (c) a political constraint entailing the execution of secondary political authority.

Only in the case of the political constraint is there involvement with a broader purpose and a generalized constituency. It is more a matter of purpose, motive, and intended effects than actual outcome. The outcome, especially in the case of the R & D spending grant, may be the same. It is the breadth of purpose (such as contributing to the national productivity versus the firm's profitability) that makes the political constraint important. This link to the public interest and to broader values distinguishes political constraints from other constraints.

According to the multi-dimensional theory, the impact of publicness on organization behavior is a function of the following factors: (1) the respective proportions of economic and political authority constraining the organization (that is, the authority mix); (2) the intensity of authority brought to bear on the organization; (3) the ability of the organization to mediate constraints via its buffering devices; (4) the authority (both political and economic) exerted by the focal organization on its environment.

Public-as-Authority Mix. Economic and political authority are not viewed as countervailing influences on the behavior of organizations, but rather as distinct influences. Increments of economic authority will be associated with: (1) increased concern for technical efficiency, (2) entrepreneur-manager oversight, (3) market valuation of labor, (4) production incentive, and (5) market-based evaluation of performance.

An infusion of political authority does not necessarily lead to a reduction in each of the above but, instead, opens the organization to an array of additional influences—influences that in some cases compete with those given above and in some instances exist side-by-side with economic influences. The influence of political authority on organization behavior varies as a function of the nature of primary and secondary political authority and as a result of the particular elements of government structures. But some of the influences are pervasive and might include such factors as: (1) increased accountability to external political actors, (2) increased interdependence, (3) concern with externalities, (4) closer ties to political cycles, (5) increased public visibility, and (6) increased concern with equity and other such prescribed social goals. These factors are suggestive, but the particular effects of political authority cannot be assessed apart from knowledge of the substantive content of primary and secondary political authority and of the pertinent governance structures. Likewise, the particular effects of economic authority cannot be assessed apart from knowledge of the substantive dimensions of the market forces in operation.

Quantity and Proportion: The Publicness Grid. At this point, the multi-dimensional theory is chiefly concerned with the *mix* of economic and political authority rather than with the *amount* of authority (although in the next chapter there is a modest attempt to deal with amount of authority). There are two reasons for the current focus. In the first place, the theory is chiefly concerned with publicness and its impacts. This is not a general theory of authority in organizations but rather a theory of publicness in which authority plays a central role. Second, and more important, the focus on mix of authority is appropriate to the level of development of the theory. A theory that fully explicated the role of authority intensity and its interactions with authority mix would, in fact, be a superior theory, but that is simply beyond the scope of this early effort.

Having presented these statements of qualification, it remains important to emphasize the fact that, whatever the mix of economic authority and political authority, some organizations will be endowed with large amounts of each while others will be endowed with small amounts of each. Figure 6.2 presents a simple "publicness grid" which locates organization types along two axes, an X-axis representing economic authority and a Y-axis representing political authority.

Figure 6.2. The Publicness Grid.

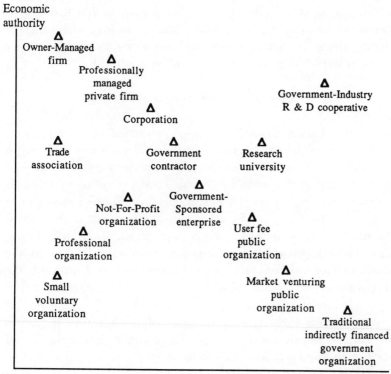

The purpose of this figure is simply to indicate that organizations, any organizations, can be arrayed according to their amount and mix of economic and political authority. It is not argued that the location of each organization type is precise. Some organization types will have a greater dispersion on the grid than will other types of organizations. For example, the location of not-for-profit organizations, an especially varied type, is particularly arbitrary. It is contended, however, that at least some of the designated organizations of each type can be expected to fall in close proximity to the icons representing its location on the grid.

If the grid looks familiar, perhaps its familiarity is owing to similar depictions of the economic character of organizations' goods and services. The difference, of course, is that this grid is based on the quality and quantity of authority affecting the organizations' behavior; thus there is no necessary correspondence to the economic character of goods and services produced.

Publicness and Organizational Processes

In Chapter One, the effect of publicness on organizations was illustrated by examining how political authority has helped shape the development of organizations in the aerospace industry. At that point, it was argued that publicness can influence virtually any aspect of organization behavior. However, it was convenient to begin by considering the effects of publicness on the "most essential" (that is, defining) processes of organizations. The multidimensional theory of publicness is developed further in the remainder of this chapter and the same tack is employed; the discussion centers on the most elemental organizational processes.

In addition to suggesting some of the implications of publicness for theoretical knowledge of organization behavior, managerial implications are explored in connection with each of the organizational processes considered.

Publicness and Resource Processes. No activity of organizations is more vital than the acquisition and management of financial resources. The essential activities of organizations presume a resource base, and much of the energy of the organization is directed toward expanding, safeguarding, or deploying resources. Also, the maintenance of the organization and its goal-directed activities is closely related to resource acquisition and management. There is a primacy to resource processes.

One difficulty in analyzing resource publicness comes quickly to mind: The scope and variety of resource processes are imposing. Among diverse organizational activities involving resources, some of the most prominent include resource acquisition, resource deployment, allocation of resources to projects and programs, and monitoring the flow of resources. Publicness can affect any or all of these resource processes (Bozeman and Strauss-man, 1983). But for conceptual analysis of resource publicness, it is best to begin with a simple but nonetheless important aspect: resource mix.

As used here, resource mix refers to the proportion of an organization's financial resources that is received from government sources. The resources might come from direct appropriations, contracts, subsidies, loans, or any of a variety of such financial vehicles.

Resource mix demonstrates the possibilities of different degrees of influence of political authority. If all private organizations were at one pole of the resource dimension (that is, receiving 100 percent of their resources from sales to private consumers in competitive markets) and all government organizations were at the other pole, there would be no need to consider the effects of publicness on the resource processes of all organizations. But organizations, including private-sector organizations, derive financial support from a variety of sources: profits from private markets, profits from government contracts, government subsidies, trust funds, user charges, special earmarked revenues, and even direct government appropriations. These sources vary in their implications for the influence of political authority.

The chief theoretical implications of resource publicness relate to the sometimes conflicting values of autonomy and stability. Organizations that remain relatively free from external constraints typically retain greater flexibility not only in managing resource processes but in strategic decision making as well. Autonomy allows the organization to adjust to the market, as conditions require, by expanding production, limiting production, initiating new products or services, stockpiling resources, creating slack resources, and so forth. Further, organizations that are not dependent on political authority can sometimes manipulate the market and in many instances create demand through advertising, aggressive marketing, expansion of sales resources, or development of new clients.

But political authority's effect on organizational resource processes is not necessarily harmful. Students of public budgeting and appropriations have shown that government organizations are not passive in their efforts to procure resources. Nor does dependence on political authority necessarily result in unpredictability of resources. In the first place, budgeting is often incremental, and, given the importance of the appropriations base, funding from political authorities usually fluctuates less than does market-based funding. Most government agencies and many government contractors plan programs assuming that appropriations will match or exceed the previous year's. Legislators, budget examiners, and executive superiors provide cues on likely appropriations outcomes, and managers are sensitive to these cues. Additionally, the budgeting process in the federal government (and many of the states) proceeds two to three years ahead of actual commitment of obligational authority. Finally, a good portion of government agency resources can be counted as "uncontrollable" in the sense that they are derived from trust funds, earmarked taxes, or indexed statutory entitlements and they involve little discretion.

The point is that political authority influence in resource acquisition is often a force for stability. Dependence can offer significant advantages. The most private firms (those sustained by profits generated from private markets) enjoy all the freedom associated with autonomy—including freedom in management and in investment of financial resources—but typically must operate in a more uncertain environment. Thus, a major implication of the publicness of organization resource processes is not intrinsically good or bad and must be judged instead in relation to management strategies and characteristics of the organization's environment. As Thompson (1967) pointed out, organizations seek strategies that shelter their core technology from environmental stress and uncertainty. In some instances, publicness is an effective shelter; in others, it is an effective shackle.

Resource publicness and management: It seems a safe bet that most businesses have more autonomy than do government agencies in the development, allocation, and use of resources. But increased publicness may well reduce the level of autonomy. By the same token, increased reliance on the market may augment the government agency's autonomy. As managers seek to diversify their funding base, some thought must be given to the possibilities for increments or decrements of decision-making autonomy likely to accompany a change in resource mix.

Resource stability often is affected by publicness. For example, Acme Widgets, Inc., enjoys success as a supplier of production inputs to manufacturers. But it just received its first major government contract, a large contract expected to virtually double its sales receipts. A change of such magnitude inevitably results in major redirections—some planned and some unplanned. One of the crucial factors for Acme's management to consider is possible long-range effects on the stability of its resource base. If Acme courts government contracts, its resource acquisition strategies will be sensitive to changes in the political climate. This means that the rules of the resource game may be changed—skill in reading market conditions (Acme's forte) doesn't imply much about skill in reading political change.

Resource publicness is changing business organizations, but resource privateness is changing many government organizations. Whether due to resource scarcity or ideology, government organizations are currently experimenting with a variety of quasi-market approaches to acquiring and managing financial resources. In many instances, there are secondary effects. Does reliance on the market undermine the stability of government organizations? Does it tend to encourage an undervaluing of socially and politically significant programs that have little market potential? These are issues for managers to ponder as they seek to change their traditional resource base.

Publicness and Organizational Life Cycles. Establishing and maintaining the organization is a basic process that is common to all organizations. Organizations come into existence, seek to maintain themselves, and ultimately perish; thus, they can be said to have life cycles. In line with the approach outlined here, organization life cycles are considered in terms of the degree to which publicness affects the creation, maintenance, and dismantling of organizations.

Government organizations depend on legal superiors for their creation. Government organizations—whether created by statute, executive order, or superior entities in the bureaucracy—are not (at least in a formal sense) self-initiating. While this formal difference between government and private organizations is important, one must also consider that business organizations rarely spring into existence all at once, unfettered by charter requirements, licensing procedures, anti-trust laws, or similar influences of political authority.

Business organizations vary considerably in regard to the effects of political authority upon their birth and death processes. Political authority rarely has major effects on the life cycles of small, voluntary organizations (except indirectly through funding support), but, at the other extreme, political authority pervades processes for the establishment and incorporation of a large firm operating in an oligarchic market and heavily constrained by anti-trust laws.

In addition to direct effects of political authority on birth and death processes, the influence of publicness results from government regulation of markets. Pfeffer (1974) provides evidence of the effects of Civil Aeronautics Board regulations on the entry of new airlines into the industry. Also, tax incentives often play an important role in the establishment of organizations (see Bozeman and Link, 1983). All of this does not imply that the formal legal differences between the creation of government and private organizations are unimportant; instead, it suggests that publicness often affects the life cycles of organizations of all types.

Life-cycle publicness and management: In all likelihood, few managers think of themselves as managing life cycles. But in fact that is exactly what is involved: developing strategies for starting new organizations, positioning the organization so it can maintain itself, and planning for the dismantling of one's own organization or another organization for which one makes policy. The publicness of life cycles intrudes on these managerial issues in several ways, but it is perhaps most prominent in decisions about the creation of new organizations.

The effect of publicness on the creation of government organizations could not be more fundamental: New government entities cannot be created without authorization from an existing government entity. But political authority can affect virtually any organization's start-up decisions. A manager-entrepreneur contemplating a new business venture might wish to scan the environment for government assistance and would find a wide array of possibilities, including, for example, state government incentive programs, Small Business Administration loan programs, government-sponsored advisory programs (such as the Retired Executive Corps), government-sponsored incubator centers, and reduced tax enterprise zones. Often publicness is of sufficient importance to alter the entrepreneur's decision calculus (which is exactly what many programs are designed to do). But the efffects of political authority are not always unidirectional. Tax rates, regulation (and deregulation), and government paperwork requirements are just a few of the products of political authority that shape go/no-go decisions of entrepreneurs and managers.

Publicness and Structural Processes

Another basic element of organizations is structure, and here, too, there are implications for publicness. There are a number of centralizing features in government that might be lumped together in the category of structural publicness. In the federal government, two of the most significant agencies in promoting structural/managerial dependence are the General Services Administration (GSA) and the Office of Management and Budget (OMB). The centralization of procurement in the GSA has no true counterpart in business organizations, although, of course, in those instances in which a single vendor dominates, there is similar dependence. The GSA has major impacts on government contractors. The OMB promulgates regulations that set management procedures for federal agencies, and, like GSA, OMB has substantial impact on the structuring and management of business organizations. Again, contractors are affected by OMB via its accounting requirements. Often, these requirements cause formidable changes in the administrative apparatus of public-sector organizations.

Structural/managerial publicness affects personnel management. Most evident are the constraints imposed by government entities on other government entities: rules and regulations concerning availability of personnel lines, hiring procedures, and civil service requirements. But many business organizations have found themselves subject to political authority in their recruitment, advancement, and management of personnel. Affirmative action and equal employment opportunity guidelines have significant impacts on business firms' hiring practices. Regulations imposed by such agencies as the Occupational Safety and Health Administration (OSHA) affect the management and direction of employees. Minimum wage legislation and social security requirements are also elements of publicness.

Organizations differ somewhat in the degree to which personnel practices are constrained. Organizations relying heavily on government contracts often find that conformance to government personnel standards is a precondition for contract awards. Universities (including private universities) are particularly vulnerable, because it is legally possible to withhold all federal money from a university because a single department or even a single project has been found in violation of affirmative action guidelines. Moreover, publicness not only has direct consequences for hiring, promotion, and personnel procedures, but it also affects the structure and operation of personnel and even line units.

Structural publicness and management: The effect of publicness on the structure of organizations often is highly visible and not well received. Indeed, the term *red tape* generally refers to rules and procedures that grow out of structural publicness. Structural publicness includes at least as many managerial issues as are encompassed by questions of red tape and bureaucratization.

As mentioned previously, the centralization of routine managerial functions (personnel management, budgeting, accounting, procurement, facilities management) in government has no true counterpart in business. However, the impacts of GAO accounting rules, OMB managerial requirements, and Office of Personnel Management (OPM) personnel rules affect many business organizations through government contracts, grants, and other business-government interactions. Sometimes managers view these elements of structural publicness as red tape, a constraint to be avoided. In many instances, this perception is surely accurate. In other instances, one man's red tape is another man's accountability mechanism. Structural publicness usually carries with it an expectation that organizational actions will be monitored, whether directly or indirectly, by public officials. "Red tape management" is a peculiar skill requiring attention to rationales, effective communication links to external actors, and a high degree of openness in decision making.

Publicness and Goal Processes

Mohr (1973) makes a distinction between transitive goals and reflexive goals. A transitive goal is "one whose referent is outside the organization in question . . . an intended impact of the organization upon its environment." Reflexive goals, by contrast, are internally oriented, deal with system maintenance, and generally involve inducements aimed at evoking member contributions to the organization: "Within the general framework of the reflexive goals, each organization works out its own rules of the game. The criteria used in partitioning organizational resources and the resultant distribution of inducements—money, power, status, psychological experience, etc.—will certainly differ from organization to organization" (Mohr, 1973, p. 476).

A distinction between government and private organizations is that the former are established with one or more transitive goals in place, usually stated in the agency's enabling legislation or executive order. As Mohr points out, private organizations may exist solely for the achievement of reflexive goals (such as the economic benefit of organization members). One of the indirect but nonetheless crucial effects of the transitive goals of government organizations pertains to public expectations. The business firm is expected to behave in its self-interest, and a narrow definition of self-interest is appropriate. However, government organizations are expected to transcend narrowly defined self-interest. If local programmatic goals conflict with broader policy goals, it is expected that the latter will prevail. This is a matter of expectation as much as reality, but the expectation itself is important in shaping behavior.

Expectations notwithstanding, students of bureaucratic politics emphasize the fact that transitive goals often are not the best guide to the behavior of public organizations. Downs (1967,

p. 2) observes, "[public] bureaucratic officials, like all other agents in society, are significantly—though not solely—motivated by their own interests." This does not, of course, imply that the public manager's goals are necessarily incompatible with the organizations' transitive goals. Downs recognizes that public managers have a "complex set of goals including power, income, prestige, security, convenience, loyalty (to an idea, an institution, or the nation), pride in excellent work, and desire to serve the public interest."

Transitive goals provide a poor guide to organizations' behavior in situations in which the goals have been displaced, ignored, or used as convenient rationalizations for reflexive goals. While government organizations can be assumed to possess formal transitive goals, it is important to remember that: (1) any organization may profess transitive goals, and (2) government/private status tells us little about the empirical significance of transitive goals.

The expectation that government organizations will seek to transcend personal and bureaucratic goals often misleads, as does the expectation that private organizations never pursue transcendent, multi-organization goals.

Goal publicness and management: Many of the managerial implications of goal publicness are related more to expectations than to formal requirements. Government organizations have goals that transcend the individual organization, and these transitive goals carry with them a public interest burden. But what about business organizations whose goals are affected by political authority? Consider the case of the engineering consulting firm paid a fee to build and then manage a county-owned solid waste disposal facility. Is the goal of the firm to make a profit from this activity? Certainly. But does the fact that the mission is a public one, authorized by political authority and monitored by public officials, affect the firm's goals? Does the firm, in effect, take on transitive goals? The answer to that question may well vary with the values of the owner-managers of particular firms. But the perceptions of the public, the attention of the mass media, and the public accountability mechanisms required by the public nature of mission are more tangible. Managers in both the public and private sectors, working in organizations whose missions and goals are affected by political authority, must be prepared to deal with a quite different and expanded organizational environment and, usually, a different set of expectations about appropriate organization behavior.

Goal publicness affects interdependence. Government managers generally assume that accomplishment of any significant goal requires the managing of interdependence. Managers in private organizations strongly affected by political authority find themselves in a similar position but often have less experience with the challenges and frustrations of seeking goals that depend on the cooperation of numerous semi-autonomous actors. Goal publicness can generate interdependence from a variety of sources. The transitive goals of government organizations (and some business organizations) ensure interdependence. The combining of public and private organization forces in joint ventures, cooperatives, and joint programming inevitably results in a degree of goal publicness and interdependence. Moreover, interdependence raises a number of managerial questions: How does one achieve transitive goals and yet balance those against existing reflexive goals and, sometimes, organizational survival? How does one cooperate and yet retain a good measure of autonomy? Profit and growth provide a useful index of private-sector organizational effectiveness (budget allocation plays a similar role in government), but how does one get a handle on the effectiveness of programs that transcend the organization?

The publicness of the organization's goals can affect managers' approaches to attaining goals. Often publicness creates greater complexity and requires the manager to cope with a range of variables over which he or she has limited control. Goal publicness presents many of the same dilemmas for private managers that public managers routinely face: attuning program accomplishment to political cycles, striving for highly visible accomplishments that impress guardians of the public purse, making bold claims for programs that might not otherwise be funded.

From Theory to Application

This chapter has included some approaches to developing a

theory of publicness. Moving from publicness concepts to publicness measures should sharpen thinking about public-private
distinctions, put additional pieces of the publicness puzzle in place,
and, along the way, yield some insights useful for policy decisions.
Publicness research is especially relevant to policy decisions for the
allocation of resources and responsibilities among organizational
types.

The next chapter illustrates a research application based on
publicness theory. Chapter Seven presents an elementary test of
publicness assumptions within the context of research and
development laboratories. R & D labs provide a useful focus in that
there is a great diversity in regard to organizational type, resource
mix, and institutional structure but, at the same time, some
similarity in organizational activities (thus providing an implicit
control for organization technology).

7

A Case Example: How the Level of Publicness Affects Performance in R & D Organizations

Research and development organizations provide a fertile ground for analysis of dimensions of publicness. There is perhaps no institutional sector with a richer variety of organization types, structures, and environments. R & D labs are located in government, universities (both public and private), and industry. Some conform to traditional government-business stereotypes, while others are at the forefront of new organizational types that are virtually impossible to classify by traditional criteria.

Modern (that is, large-scale, bureaucratized) R & D laboratories have existed for less than 100 years and during that time have evolved from the relatively homogeneous, product-driven, technical shops of the nineteenth century to today's highly diverse set of research performers (Dupree, 1957; Mowery, 1981). Research organizations of immense importance to national productivity, innovation, and security are found in both government and industry. Such industrial laboratories as American Telephone and Telegraph (AT&T) Bell Laboratories and the International Business Machines (IBM) Watson Research Center are similar in

Note: This chapter, written with Michael Crow, draws from Crow and Bozeman, forthcoming-a, and forthcoming-b.

107

scope and size to such federal installations as the Oak Ridge National Laboratory.

The Department of Energy national laboratories (for example, Oak Ridge, Argonne, Brookhaven) are particularly interesting from the standpoint of the publicness puzzle. Oak Ridge, for instance, is a federal government laboratory that is managed by a corporation (Martin Marietta Corporation) and that produces a variety of research, including nuclear research aimed almost exclusively at the federal government, basic and applied research for the public domain, and, more recently, research that can be patented by business firms. The ambiguous status of Oak Ridge is further complicated by research partnerships with industry and facilities-sharing programs. Nor are the national laboratories solely responsible for the increasing confusion of organizational types and the blurring of sectors. The Department of Defense's Independent Research and Development (IRAD) organizations are owned by private firms but are totally or largely financed by government. And as government laboratories dabble in the marketplace—selling patents, setting up industrial parks and incubators, encouraging industrial spin-off firms—the distinction between business and government research organizations becomes even more tenuous.

The changing environment of R & D organizations is common knowledge among science policy analysts, but the traditional distinctions between government and business research organizations continue to dominate much of the thinking about the allocation of resources and responsibilities among R & D providers. In part, the business-government distinctions continue to be used simply as a convenient shorthand. More to the point, there are important differences, at least in aggregate, between business and government laboratories. However, the purpose of the analysis presented here is to compare the government-industry stereotype to an approach based on the dimensions of publicness model.

In this chapter, 250 R & D organizations are classified according to both traditional legal status criteria for public-private distinction and a measure of publicness based chiefly on percentage of government financing. This taxonomic effort serves several purposes. After determining the degree of divergence between traditional classification and a dimensional concept of publicness, a publicness-privateness typology is formulated and tested by a case study analysis of thirty-two R & D organizations. The results illustrate the possibilities for alternatives to traditional thinking about public-private distinctions. Implications of the case studies for organizational effectiveness are discussed. Finally, some of the more general implications of the analysis are considered and research strategies are outlined.

A Study in Organizational Diversity: The National Comparative R & D Laboratory Project

The National Comparative R & D Laboratory Project (NCRL) is an ongoing research project aimed at understanding the diversity in the environments, organizational structures, policies, and performance of research organizations in the United States (Crow, 1985; Loveless, 1985; Crow and Bozeman, forthcoming-a, forthcoming-b; Bozeman and Loveless, forthcoming). The project focuses particularly on the differences between public and private research organizations. But whereas previous studies examining differences between public and private labs (such as Marcson, 1960, 1972; Fusfeld and Langlois, 1982) have focused almost exclusively on simple binary distinctions based on formal legal status, NCRL studies examine R & D organizations according to a dimensional concept of publicness and privateness.

Classifying the Organizational Population

Approximately 829 R & D organizations in North America are involved in energy-related research. These comprise the organizational population for this analysis. The focus on organizations working in the same broad field is beneficial for a study interested in isolating the impact of publicness. Often public-private comparisons are handicapped by an inability to sort out the effects of sector from effects produced by differences (obviously not randomly distributed) in products, goods, and services.

Table 7.1. Classification by Ownership of the Study Population.

Ownership class	Number of units	Category description
Industrial	258 (31.1%)	Laboratory facilities are owned by an industrial organization.
Government	74 (8.9%)	Laboratory facilities and programs are owned and operated by an agency of the government.
Cooperative	414 (49.9%)	Laboratory facilities and programs are cooperatively owned and operated by more than one organizational type.
Mixed	83 (10%)	Portions of the laboratory's facilities and programs are owned by an industrial concern or university and portions are owned by a government agency.
Total	829 (100%)	

NCRL's analysis of the legal status of the 829 R & D facilities indicated that 74 (8.9 percent) are owned and operated by government and thus are easily classified as government organizations. However, one cannot assume that the remaining 90 percent are industrial organizations. Indeed, only 258 (31.1 percent) are easily classified as industrial organizations in the sense that they are entirely privately owned and managed. As Table 7.1 indicates, the *majority* of the organization population cannot be meaningfully classified as government or industry.

Classifying the Publicness of R & D Organizations

A binary classification (government-industry) is of limited utility for the variegated environment of energy R & D organizations. An expanded fourfold classification seems more meaningful but contributes little to an understanding of the role of publicness among the organizations. A simple dimensional scheme is employed here as an alternative to more conventional views of the publicness of organizations. The scheme involves only two variables and quite simple measures.

The Publicness Measure. Any of a variety of publicness measures is consistent with the assumptions presented in Chapter Six. However, several criteria can be identified to assist in the selection of a specific measure. At this preliminary stage, a straightforward, uncomplicated measure seems most appropriate, one that is easily measured, has face validity, and is applicable to virtually any organization. The measure employed here is the percentage of the organization's financial resources received from government sources. This measure is taken as a proxy for political authority. While there is surely no one-to-one correspondence between government resources and government (much less public) control, there is at least some reason to believe, as suggested in Chapter Five, that endowment and constraints rooted ultimately in political authority shape the organization and affect its behavior.

A measure of percentage of government financing yields interval-level data, but in the interests of conservatism and in light of the desire to create a useful typology, a threefold classification was employed, as follows:

High publicness = 76 to 100 percent of R & D program funding from government sources

Moderate publicness = 26 to 75 percent of R & D program funding from government sources

Low publicness = 0 to 25 percent of R & D program funding from government sources

These categories are, of course, somewhat arbitrary, but they do provide a beginning point for seeking empirical differences according to a dimensional concept of publicness. Additional measures have been suggested elsewhere (see Bozeman, 1984; Bozeman and Loveless, forthcoming).

The Privateness Measure. As a proxy for economic
authority, the products and services of the R & D laboratory are
measured in terms of expressed market orientation. At one
extreme, an R & D product can be directed toward public domain
science and technology for the broad benefit of society and with no
one group benefiting more than another from the product. So-
called basic research ("knowledge for its own sake") is usually
thought of in this way. At the other extreme, R & D products can
be aimed directly at the market with a single organization reaping
full benefit by capturing all the profit associated with the good or
service (in other words, excluding all but paying customers from
use of the good). Applied research and development activity,
generally speaking, is more closely tied to market needs and
signals.

Three categories measure the degree of market focus (that is,
importance of "economic authority") for the organization:

Generic R & D product = "pure research" aimed at the public
domain with little market concern;
the chief product is a physical or
(more often) intellectual property
having the characteristics of a public
good.

Balanced R & D product = balance of market-directed and public domain R & D products. R & D is
dominated by neither proprietary
aims nor "pure research."

Proprietary R & D product = Chief concern is with developing
products for the market; products
have the economic character of private goods.

It is important to note that virtually all of the organizations
included in this study are involved in some mix of activities,
typically carrying out at least some basic research and at least some
research driven by and targeted to near-term payoff in the market.

Nevertheless, classification presented relatively few problems. Researchers classified the organizations into one of the three categories; consultation with R & D managers participating in the study indicated nearly complete agreement about classification (see Crow and Bozeman, forthcoming-a, for classification details).

A Publicness Typology

To facilitate classification, a survey instrument was constructed to derive information about the organizations' environmental contexts, structures, and resource flows. The questionnaire was mailed to laboratory directors of the energy R & D laboratories; 250 usable (that is, filled out in full) questionnaires were received from participants. Each of the participating 250 R & D organizations was classified according to the two measures discussed above. Variance was distributed among the categories in such a way as to enable analysis by a three-by-three matrix. Table 7.2 presents the resultant publicness classification and introduces the names (subsequently discussed in more detail) developed for the organization types associated with each of the nine cells. Table 7.3 provides additional information as to time of origin, funding levels, and stated planning horizon.

The results of this survey should not be taken as an accurate representation of the distribution of organization types generally or even for the population of energy R & D organizations. Comparison of sample figures to population figures (see Crow, 1985) indicates that Public Generic laboratories (the government lab stereotype) are statistically overrepresented and Independent Market laboratories (the industry lab stereotype) are underrepresented. However, our purpose is not estimation of proportions of lab types but determination of correspondence of the publicness typology with the more conventional fourfold scheme based on legal status (ownership type). Table 7.4 provides a cross-tabulation of R & D product type (privateness) according to the fourfold scheme.

To some extent, the findings given in Table 7.4 are subject to different interpretations. Clearly, the government-industry ster-

Table 7.2. Classification of R & D Organizations by Environmental Influence.

Level of governmental influence

Level of market influence (Nature of R & D products)	High	Moderate	Low
Generic product (low) Total % Total	Public generic 121 (49.4)	Quasi-Public generic 40 (16.3)	Independent generic 6 (2.4)
Balanced product (moderate)	Public Multi-Market 4 (1.6)	Quasi-Public Multi-Market 11 (4.5)	Independent Multi-Market 10 (4.1)
Proprietary product (high)	Public Market 10 (4.1)	Quasi-Public Market 11 (4.5)	Independent Market 32 (13.1)

Number of missing observations = 5

Table 7.3. Laboratory Characteristics by Various Levels of Environmental Influence.

Level of government influence (publicness)

Level of market influence (Nature of R & D products)	High	Moderate	Low
Generic	**Public Generic** N = 121 A = 1958 F = $2.95 GI = 2.13 Obj = 5.68	**Quasi-Public Generic** N = 40 A = 1957 F = $1.2 GI = 2.52 Obj = 5.30	**Independent Generic** N = 6 A = 1953 F = $.753 GI = 3.83 Obj = 4.4
Balanced	**Public Multi-Market** N = 4 A = 1961 F = $.692 GI = 2.29 Obj = 5.75	**Quasi-Public Multi-Market** N = 11 A = 1958 F = $2.0 GI = 3.27 Obj = 3.36	**Independent Multi-Market** N = 10 A = 1940 F = $8.4 GI = 4.8 Obj = 2.1
Proprietary	**Public Market** N = 10 A = 1959 F = $5.65 GI = 2.5 Obj = 4.3	**Quasi-Public Market** N = 11 A = 1957 F = $1.5 GI = 3.18 Obj = 2.18	**Independent Market** N = 30 A = 1953 F = $6.795 GI = 4.75 Obj = 1.63

Key: N = number of observations

A = average year of laboratory start-up

F = median annual funding (millions of dollars)

GI = average level of government influence, where 1 = dependent and 5 = independent

Obj = research objectives of laboratory, where 1 = short-range applied and 8 = long-range basic research

Table 7.4. Nature of R & D Product by Classical Ownership Groups.

	Generic	Balanced	Proprietary	Row total
Industrial	6	11	29	46 (18.8%)
Government agency	31	2	6	39 (15.9%)
Cooperative	114	9	14	137 (55.9%)
Mixed	16	3	4	23 (9.4%)
Column total (100.0%)	167 (68.1%)	25 (10.2%)	53 (21.6%)	245

Note: Number of missing observations = 5

eotypes are not entirely accurate when 39 percent of the industry labs are engaged in producing goods and services not primarily driven by market concerns and when 15 percent of government labs are engaged in predominantly market-driven research. However, one might easily argue that, in aggregate, the old stereotypes serve quite well. And an examination focusing exclusively on government and industry labs seems to support such an argument. However, the stereotypes offer little help in interpreting the behavior and goals of the majority of labs, the majority that are neither pure type industry nor pure type government.

The question remains, however, as to the behavioral consequences, if any, of the publicness classification scheme. For example, are Public Generic industry labs more like other Public Generic labs or more like other industry labs? What effects, if any, does strong market involvement seem to have on government labs? The answer to such questions goes beyond simple taxonomic exercises. Case studies undertaken as part of the NCRL project shed some light on the behavioral significance of publicness.

Case Studies of the Publicness Typology

Intensive on-site case studies were performed for thirty-two of the energy R & D organizations, including at least two in each of the nine cells of the publicness typology. The case studies were aimed at determining whether differences existed among (and within) cell types, with no strong expectation as to the direction of those differences. The overall goal of the case research was to determine whether the matrix discriminated organization behaviors and attributes. The variables of interest included: (1) organization history; (2) organization structure; (3) resource flows; (4) planning formats; (5) R & D objectives; (6) scope of R & D activities. In each of the thirty-two research facilities visited, a common semi-structured interview schedule was employed (Crow and Bozeman, forthcoming-a, forthcoming-b) in meetings with the lab director(s) and other top R & D management personnel. Interviews were followed by a tour of the facility and follow-up telephone calls.

The discussion presented below is according to cell type (for example, Public Generic, Public Market, and so on). In each case, the discussion draws from all the cases, but the conclusions are not (for brevity's sake) directly tied to the data. For an expanded discussion linking conclusions more closely to the data, see Crow (1985) and Crow and Bozeman (forthcoming-a). For each of the cell types, a table is presented describing the organizations but using apocryphal names.

Public Generic. In terms of the publicness taxonomy, Public Generic research organizations are high on publicness (that is, they have a high percentage of government financing) and low on privateness (their products are targeted to the public domain). Table 7.5 provides summary data for the five Public Generic cases.

Public Generic research organizations are characterized by national leadership in one or many scientific and technological fields and by close involvement with the federal government in terms of setting and carrying out national research agendas. Public Generic labs generally are stable, and this stability is one of the reasons they play a prominent role in the national research agenda. The Public Generics have many of the characteristics of the stereotypical government laboratory, but Public Generics are found in a variety of environmental settings. Among the cases considered here (Table 7.5), one is an industry lab, one government, one mixed, and two are cooperative.

Table 7.5. Public Generic Laboratories Case Study Characteristics.

	Classical ownership	Lab funding	Total lab staff	Annual approx. budget ($ in millions)	Research frontier	Research planning	Organizational stability	Organizational structure
Acme Aviation	Industrial	1956	75	$ 4.5	Basic	Multi-year time frame	Very stable	Separate research facility of a parent corporation with research facilities in various operating units
Energy Pollution Research Laboratory	Government	1975	85	$ 9.5	Basic & applied	Multi-year planning	Somewhat stable	One of several labs operated by the parent company
Institute for Advanced Energy Research	Mixed	1947	541	$19.0	Basic	Five-year research planning and one-year programming and budgeting	Very stable	Principal investigator-led research group; discipline based
Laser Science Center	Cooperative	1949	80	$ 3.3	Basic	Five-year research planning and one-year programming and budgeting	Very stable	Principal investigator-led research group; discipline based
The Neutron Institute	Cooperative	1938	167	$ 7.7	Basic	Five-year research planning and one-year programming and budgeting	Very stable	Principal investigator-led research group; discipline based

There are two major subtypes among the Public Generics, including government-owned and -operated facilities and federalized institutions with much governmental interdependence. In both cases, the government, through formal authority, agreements, and/or resource dependence, exercises some control over the laboratory. Moreover, there is considerable variation in the depth of government influence on the Public Generic labs. Some organizations, such as the Energy Pollution Research Laboratory, have limited scientific autonomy, while in others, such as the Laser Science Center, the government sets only the broadest guidelines, and even these are subject to considerable influence by the lab. It is clear, however, that for all the Public Generics the government has a critical role in establishing the broad outlines of the scientific agenda.

Quasi-Public Generic. The Quasi-Public Generic receives a substantial portion of its budget (though not as much as the Public Generic) from the federal government and, like the Public Generic, is engaged in research chiefly directed to the public domain. The typical Quasi-Public Generic actively pursues government research dollars. This contrasts again with the Public Generic in the sense that the government comes to the Public Generic (which is invariably an R & D facility of major importance) while the Quasi-Public Generic typically goes to the federal government and other resource providers seeking to sell its technical skills. Table 7.6 summarizes information about the Quasi-Public Generic.

There is much variation among the Quasi-Public Generics, partly because there is (with only a few exceptions) no stable research mission. Each of the organizations offers its research services, specialized instruments and equipment, and skilled personnel to any interested contract provider. Long-range planning is uncommon. Thus, research tends to be piecemeal and noncumulative and the labs generally are much less stable than are the Public Generics. The market alternatives of the Quasi-Public Generic serve to mix economic and political authority; thus, the Quasi-Public Generics can be said to have a moderate level of publicness. The influence of political authority takes various

Table 7.6. Quasi-Public Generic Laboratories Case Study Characteristics.

	Classical ownership	Lab funding	Total lab staff	Annual approx. budget ($ in millions)	Research frontier	Research planning	Organizational stability	Organizational structure
Magnetic Science Center	Cooperative (jointly owned and operated by a university and an agency)	1949	32	$1.35	Applied	One-year planning horizon	Very stable	Fluid, organized around principal investigator-led research group
California Cyclotron Center	Cooperative (jointly owned and operated by a university and an agency)	1970	35	$1.2	Applied	Annual to biannual basis	Unstable	Organized around topical research groups
Energy Research, Inc.	Mixed (the facilities are partially owned by a private research company and various agencies of the government)	1966	110	$9.0	Applied and development	Little research planning	Unstable	Organized around topical research groups
Institute for Solar System Development	Cooperative (jointly owned and operated by a university and an agency)	1972	39	$1.5	Applied and development	Annual or biannual basis	Unstable	Organized around topical research groups

forms. Consider the case of Energy Research, Inc. This R & D organization had its origins in industry but evolved to a point at which its legal status is mixed, including some formal control and management by government. For Energy Research, Inc., political authority has influenced personnel decisions in both hiring and project assignment, but it has not much affected the substance of particular research projects.

Independent Generic. The Independent Generic, like the two lab types previously discussed, focuses chiefly on public domain–targeted basic research. But the Independent Generic does not work closely with government and is not strongly influenced by political authority. The Independent Generic is low on both publicness and privateness scores (market influence) and, as one might expect, is not a common type (6 of 245 labs, or 2.4 percent). In terms of conventional expectations about the roles of public and private labs, the Independent Generic is an anomaly. Table 7.7 provides information about the Independent Generics included in the case studies.

There is considerable variety among the Independent Generics. Regarding research missions, there may be less in common among the Independent Generic labs than any other type. Each is a unique entity focusing on a narrow and highly specialized research agenda. Independent Generics chart their own course with little concern for either the government or the market. It is not surprising that their resource levels are generally lower than are those for other lab types. At least among research organizations, autonomy has its drawbacks, particularly with respect to funding levels. Generally, the base of support is decentralized, with much of the responsibility for acquiring resources falling on the shoulders of research personnel. The Independent Generics seek to create an open environment with maximum scientific freedom for their research personnel. But this often means that the individual researchers, due to lack of stable external support, also must devote considerable attention to entrepreneurial activities.

In the case of the Indiana Institute and the Chemical Processing Institute, the organizations were created out of a desire for a new type of organizational form to support research. The

Table 7.7. Independent Generic Laboratories Case Study Characteristics.

	Classical ownership	Lab funding	Total lab staff	Annual approx. budget ($ in millions)	Research frontier	Research planning	Organizational stability	Organizational structure
Chemical Processing Institute	Cooperative (jointly owned and operated by a university and several industrial partners)	1983	10	$ .2	Applied and development	Two-year planning horizon	Somewhat unstable	Principal investigator-led research groups
The Indiana Institute	Cooperative (jointly owned and operated by several family foundations)	1970	50	$1.6	Applied and some basic	Annual to biannual basis	Unstable	A loose federation of principal investigator-led research groups
Center for Advanced Energy Physics	Cooperative (jointly owned and operated by a university and several agencies)	1957	43	$2.4	Applied and some basic	Annual to biannual basis	Very unstable	A loose federation of principal investigator-led research groups

Chemical Processing Institute is a cooperatively owned research facility operated (not owned) by a university. The Indiana Institute was begun with funds from private, industrial, and government sources and was established as a cooperative. Independent Generics are typically created outside either government or industry. Both organizations have managed to retain a high degree of autonomy and a good measure of control over the research agenda. They have accomplished this by relying heavily on the initiative of individual scientific investigators and, to some extent, sacrificing program breadth.

Public Multi-Market. The most uncommon organization type in the sample, the Public Multi-Market, receives a high percentage of its resources from government but produces a balanced mix of products, some aimed for the market, some for public domain science. Public Multi-Markets are not only uncommon but also small; their average funding levels are lower than those of any other organizational type, and they tend to have smaller staffs and fewer programs. Additional information about the Public Multi-Markets is given in Table 7.8.

Only two site visits were made to Public Multi-Market organizations (there were only four from which to choose, and two declined to participate in the case study component of the research). The State Energy Lab is a state-government–owned and –operated facility with a broad research agenda in fields related to natural resources. The Atomic Energy Laboratory is a federal laboratory operated under a charter with a government corporation. Its primary research mission is in the area of nuclear research. The analysis of only two cases is limiting, but it is worth noting that the two cases have much in common. Both organizations operate under the general auspices of a government agency and deliver a wide range of scientific and technical services in addition to standard research investigations. In both cases, the lab was established to meet a public need for technical services. The labs are not stable in terms of either resource base or structure. The program focus is parochial, with only modest contribution to national scientific needs. Generally, the focus is on applied and development work, but for a public client. There is, however,

Table 7.8. Public Multi-Market Laboratories Case Study Characteristics.

	Classical ownership	Lab funding	Total lab staff	Annual approx. budget ($ in millions)	Research frontier	Research planning	Organizational stability	Organizational structure
The State Energy Lab	Governmental	1970	37	$ .75	Research information produced used to assist in the application of new technological alternatives. Technical services and applied	Biannual basis	Unstable	Hierarchical and department based
The Atomic Energy Laboratory	Governmental	1944	2,360	$133.5	With a one- to ten-year time horizon, research focuses on technological frontier. Applied	Biannual basis	Somewhat unstable	Hierarchical, technology-based departments

some market influence (often at the behest of the government sponsor), and the market influence often diffuses the activity of the lab and results in conflict and cross purposes. The impact of political authority is strongly felt in each lab, with chief government sponsors exerting wide-ranging control over both technical and management issues.

Quasi-Public Multi-Market. The Quasi-Public Multi-Market is similar in some respects to the Public Multi-Market: Some products are aimed at the market, and some are not. However, the impact of political authority on the Quasi-Public Multi-Market is much less than on the Public Multi-Market. Perhaps as a result (perhaps as a cause), the organization structures and legal statuses are much more varied. For example, the three cases include a government-chartered, university-operated, cooperatively owned facility (the Magnetic Transport Center), an industrially owned facility financed by government research and profits from activities related to its government research (General Energy, Inc.), and a cooperatively owned and operated facility based at a university (Institute of Superconductivity). Additional information is given in Table 7.9.

Quasi-Public Multi-Markets are best characterized as specialized research facilities designed to meet particularistic needs of both government and industry. The three R & D organizations examined here retain considerable autonomy in setting goals and research agendas. Rather than "chasing" dollars by agreeing to provide any of a wide range of scientific and technical services, the Quasi-Public Multi-Markets have an area of expertise, and they seek to deliver it to a broad, diverse market. General Energy, Inc., is much larger than either of the other two organizations, but there are many similarities among the three. The two smaller facilities resemble the more or less autonomous departments of General Energy, Inc. Since Quasi-Public Multi-Markets sell research projects (not integrated programs) to meet particular needs, they tend to play an important part in responding to a national research agenda but have very little role in framing the agenda. Quasi-Public Multi-Markets serve both government and industry without close integration or even especially close ties to either.

Table 7.9. Quasi-Public Multi-Market Laboratories Case Study Characteristics.

	Classical ownership	Lab funding	Total lab staff	Annual approx. budget ($ in millions)	Research frontier	Research planning	Organizational stability	Organizational structure
The Magnetic Transport Center	Cooperative (owned and operated by a university, several industries, and several agencies)	1970	17	$ 4.2	Applied	One- to two-year planning	Stable	Principal investigator-led research groups organized within a hierarchical structure
General Energy, Inc.	Industrial	1955	1,781	$150.0	Research focuses on developing new applications for options on the technological frontier and new permutations of various combinations of the various options. Time horizon five to thirty years. Applied and some basic	Two-year time frame	Very stable	Topically structured departments with principal investigator-led research groups
Institute of Super-conduc-tivity	Cooperative (owned and operated by a university and several industrial and government units)	1970	40	$ 1.4	Applied and basic	Irregular planning results in a research agenda marketed to interested parties	Stable	Principal investigator-led research groups

Independent Multi-Market. The Independent Multi-Market has a balanced orientation to the market (that is, intermediate privateness) and a minimal degree of political authority and control (low publicness). In some instances, it seems that the Independent Multi-Market has an interest in devoting some of its resources and energies to the production of basic research and public domain science, but a strong market orientation and, often, control by a parent organization get in the way of a more balanced approach. The result is that the Independent Multi-Market is characterized by organizational instability and some confusion of objectives. A profile of the four Independent Multi-Markets included in the case analysis is presented in Table 7.10.

The lack of government influence on these research organizations has not been an unmitigated blessing. Independent Multi-Markets are more vulnerable to downturns in the economy than are most types of research organizations. Most organizations, and particularly those producing at least some generic or public domain scientific products, can rely on government largess even in the face of lean markets. This is especially true, of course, if some of the goods produced are deemed to be in the national interest. The pattern exhibited in most of the Independent Multi-Markets is that upturns in economic conditions lead to an increase in public domain science and technology and downturns lead to a shift toward a greater proportion of proprietary research. In part, this is because public domain research is viewed as an activity to be indulged in during periods of resource munificence—an activity that can go by the boards once resources begin to decline.

Each of the Independent Multi-Markets was begun as a facility providing technical service either to a broad industrial sector or to a large industrial firm (although this does not imply that they are all industrial labs). However, each of the labs has grown to a point at which there is an interest in pursuing long-range research objectives. Typically, the day-to-day technical services and product modification demands placed on the labs have proved an obstacle to pursuit of longer-range objectives. Only Photo Chemicals, Inc., has succeeded in developing and implementing a long-range R & D plan. But even here research managers report

Table 7.10. Independent Multi-Market Laboratories Case Study Characteristics.

	Classical ownership	Lab funding	Total lab staff	Annual approx. budget ($ in millions)	Research frontier	Research planning	Organizational stability	Organizational structure
Ewing Oil R & D, Inc.	Industrial	1956	100	$6.1	Development	Annual basis	Unstable	Departmentally structured around products of the firm
Photo Chemicals, Inc.	Industrial	1971	101	$9.2	Development, some applied	Annual basis	Unstable	Departmentally structured around products of the firm
Seattle Tech., Inc.	Industrial	1940	12	$1.0	Although the lab does have the desire to contribute to the generic technology base, it can be fairly stated that all or most of its work occurs on the achievement frontier. Time horizon is six months or less to two years. Development, some applied	Annual basis	Unstable	Departmentally structured around products of the firm
Mineral Research Laboratories, Inc.	Mixed (privately owned with joint operating contracts)	1961	125	$7.5	Development, some applied	Project basis with the individual contracting firms	Very unstable	Departmentally structured with semi-independent investigators

that a decline in strength of the parent company's product line could cause the derailment of the long-range R & D programs.

Public Market. Public Market labs are in direct contrast to expectations about proprietary-focused labs: They seek to produce products aimed directly at the market but are strongly influenced by government and receive most of their funding from government sources. Most of the Public Market labs are industrial research institutes in the European tradition: government financing in pursuit of industrial R & D goals. As one might imagine, the Public Market labs are beset with organizational conflict. Table 7.11 provides summary information.

Unlike the Public Generics, which are funded with broad-scale program budgets and retain considerable discretion in allocation of funds, the Public Market labs are funded on a project-by-project basis. The lack of a base and long-term support has contributed to organizational instability. As a result, long-term planning is uncommon and research proceeds in fits and starts. Perhaps more than any other organization type, the Public Market lab is sensitive to external environmental changes. Changes in the political climate can have immediate consequences. But, since the labs serve industrial objectives, changes in market, product, or technologies also can have deep immediate impacts. Both Southwest Mining Laboratory and the Provincial Mining Laboratory are closely tied to the minerals industry and suffered dramatically from industry slowdowns in the early 1980s. Both were, in fact, to be dismantled, but their publicness served them well. The Southwest Mining Laboratory, through direct involvement in the political process, secured sufficient funds to maintain the lab during a period of decline. The Provincial Mining Laboratory maneuvered to redefine its mission from intermediate-term R & D to short-term R & D and thereby managed to survive, if not flourish.

Quasi-Public Market. In the Quasi-Public Market there is shared financing of product development and technical services. The Quasi-Public Market is much like the stereotypical industry lab except that a significant portion of its budget comes from government. Table 7.12 profiles the Quasi-Public Market cases.

Table 7.11. Public Market Laboratories Case Study Characteristics.

	Classical ownership	Lab funding	Total lab staff	Annual approx. budget ($ in millions)	Research frontier	Research planning	Organizational stability	Organizational structure
Southwest Mining Laboratory	Government	1962	117	$ 5.3	Development	Follows government budget cycle. Two-year time frame	Unstable	Technology-based divisions
The Provincial Mining Laboratory	Government	1969	135	$ 5.1	Development	Follows government budget cycle. Two-year time frame	Unstable	Technology-based divisions
Advanced Population Laboratory	Government	1972	130	$ 6.0	Development	Follows government budget cycle. Two-year time frame	Unstable	Technology-based divisions
Underwater Energy Systems Center	Cooperative (jointly owned and operated by a university and an agency)	1945	245	$16.0	Development	Follows government budget cycle. Two-year time frame	Stable	Technology-based divisions and some principal investigator-led groups

Table 7.12. Quasi-Public Market Laboratories Case Study Characteristics.

	Classical ownership	Lab funding	Total lab staff	Annual approx. budget ($ in millions)	Research frontier	Research planning	Organizational stability	Organizational structure
Energy Engineering, Inc.	Industrial	1976	25	$1.25	Development, some applied	Annual basis and follows general product marketing cycles	Somewhat unstable	Divisions organized around products
Regional Energy Research Center	Mixed (owned in part by a university and in part by a government with industrial funding)	1967	15	$ .4	Development	Project basis	Very unstable	Projects with loose divisional structure
Advanced Turbine Research	Industrial	1958	26	$2.0	Development, some applied	Annual basis and follows general product marketing cycles	Unstable	Divisions organized around products

There is some considerable variation among the three Quasi-Public Markets analyzed here. Energy Engineering, Inc., is an industry lab spun off from a major research university. The Regional Energy Research Center has mixed ownership status, is housed at a university, and is a government-chartered research facility. Advanced Turbine Research is a more traditional industrial laboratory in most ways, except that much of its research is financed by government. The key link among these diverse organizational types is the government's support for a proprietary product. And this shared characteristic seems to have important implications. Each of the organizations enjoys a relatively low level of organizational risk as a result of significant government financing and often has the ability to generate some slack resources. Still, government is kept somewhat at a distance so that the operation of the facility is subject more to market forces than to changes in the political climate. There is some instability but not nearly so much as with the Public Markets. The labs in the case studies are all driven by a single or a single class of R & D product. Instability results chiefly from market shifts related to the demand for the product.

Independent Market. The archetype industrial R & D lab, the Independent Market, has little or no government financing and, at least in the cases considered, very little government influence. They serve the firm by producing research that can lead quickly to products or product modification. Table 7.13 provides summary information about the Independent Market research organization.

Some of the Independent Markets (for example, the Smith Chemical Research Laboratory and Power Systems Laboratory, Inc.) have a long-range research program, but it is subservient to short-term needs. In each of the facilities, there is significant control outside the laboratory, and research is strongly influenced by marketing staff and customers. Lab personnel often play the role of "technical firefighter," responding to alarms coming in from the outside. Invariably, the Independent Markets are closely integrated with other operating units of the firm. There is some research planning, but it is for short-term applied projects, and

Table 7.13. Independent Market Laboratories Case Study Characteristics.

	Classical ownership	Lab funding	Total lab staff	Annual approx. budget ($ in millions)	Research frontier	Research planning	Organizational stability	Organizational structure
Power Systems Laboratory, Inc.	Industrial	1947	663	$40.0	Applied and development	Formalized annual program planning	Stable	Product/process-oriented research divisions
Smith Chemical Research Laboratory	Industrial	1961	120	$ 6.6	Applied and development	Formalized annual program planning	Stable	Product/process-oriented research divisions
Black Forest Energy Lab, Inc.	Industrial	1976	20	$ 1.75	Applied and development	Formalized annual program planning	Somewhat unstable	Product/process-oriented research divisions
Metalville Research Center	Industrial	1947	400	$25.0	Applied and development	Formalized annual program planning	Stable	Product/process-oriented research divisions

planning is a joint process involving several units within the firm. The Independent Markets tend to be quite stable, well funded, and not as tied to the profits-loss statement of the firm as one might expect.

Summary Findings

The findings resulting from the interviews at the case study sites are presented in Table 7.14. In this section, findings are discussed according to category of organization attribute or behavior.

Research Scope. Public Generic laboratories and Quasi-Public Multi-Market laboratories have a national research scope. That is, research at these labs is responsive to the broadest of scientific questions and is a national resource. In each of the other organization types, the research agenda is largely directed to the needs of the parent organization(s).

Public Generic laboratories, because of their national orientation, stable funding, and minimal market influences, have been able to operate on the scientific and technological frontier. Quasi-Public Multi-Market laboratories address research of national importance but usually on a more narrow base and with more applied problems. For both groups, the research agenda is set more by external scientific and technical change than by either political or economic influences. The agendas of all the other organization types tend to be as responsive to political and market change as to scientific developments.

Type of Technical Change. Both Public Generic and Quasi-Public Multi-Market laboratories pursue self-determined research programs. As a result, they are less directed toward well-defined, evolutionary technical change. While the high publicness level experienced by Public Generic laboratories precludes total independence, it is important to note that these laboratories were federalized *because* of their independent ongoing research programs. For the Public Generics, political authority is more an endowment than a constraint.

Table 7.14. Organizational Variation by R & D Organization Type.

	Public Generic	Quasi-Public Generic	Independent Generic	Public Multi-Market	Quasi-Public Multi-Market	Independent Multi-Market	Public Market	Quasi-Public Market	Independent Market
Research Scope	National Interfirm	Regional Intrafirm	Regional Intrafirm	Regional Intrafirm	National Interfirm	Regional Intrafirm	Regional Intrafirm	Regional Intrafirm	Regional Intrafirm
Type of Technical Change Pursued	Revolutionary	Evolutionary	Evolutionary	Evolutionary	Revolutionary	Evolutionary	Evolutionary	Evolutionary	Evolutionary and sometimes revolutionary
Research Frontier	Scientific and technological	Achievement and technological	Technological and scientific	Technological	Technological and scientific	Achievement	Achievement	Achievement	Achievement and technological
Technological Research Planning	Multi-Year	Annual to biennial	Annual to biennial	Biennial	Annual to biennial	Annual	Annual to biennial	Annual	Annual
Organizational Stability	Stable	Unstable	Unstable	Unstable	Stable	Unstable	Unstable	Unstable	Stable
Organizational Structure	Principal Investigator Mode	Principal Investigator Mode	Principal Investigator Mode	Departmental	Departmental and Principal Investigator Mode	Departmental	Departmental	Departmental	Departmental

Other laboratory types are more oriented toward well-defined and even predictable research focused on narrower scientific problems. This is especially the case for the Independent Multi-Market laboratories. The fact that they rely almost totally on parent organization funding means that first and foremost their research is directed toward linear improvement of existing products and/or processes. During those periods when nonlinear technical alternatives can be pursued, there is always some tension with research objectives arising from day-to-day problems.

Research Planning. Four basic variations regarding research planning occur among the nine types of R & D laboratories identified. Public Generic laboratories are unique in that their planning horizons are generally greater than three years.

High-publicness environments seem to result in longer-range and more formalized planning. This tendency is intensified as the R & D product becomes more generic. Environments with lower levels of publicness generally only plan on an annual basis and even then are subject to rapid, market-induced changes in plans in the Independent Multi-Market and Quasi-Public Market laboratories.

Organizational Stability. Three types of stability were examined here, including number and extent of budget fluctuations, program change, and life cycle threats. Generally, stability is a function of high publicness in generic laboratories, low publicness in proprietary (market-directed) laboratories, and moderate publicness among mixed-market labs. In other words, laboratory stability appears to come either with a clear mission and a single funding source, as in the cases of Public Generic and Independent Market laboratories, or with a self-determined course with balanced products and funding as illustrated by the Quasi-Public Multi-Market laboratories. As expected, program funding leads to greater stability and project funding leads to less.

Organizational Structure. The impact of the market (R & D product) is the key determinant affecting the structure of the R & D laboratory. The more proprietary the product, the more organization tends to be departmental and centralized, even bureaucratic. Laboratory types with more generic R & D are more decentralized, typically organized around individual scientists and their research groups.

Summary Hypotheses. While the case study data do not permit definitive conclusions about R & D organizations, some hypotheses are strongly suggested. These hypotheses would not easily emerge from an analysis based on more conventional treatment of public-private distinctions.

1. The production of generic research in a stable environment requires high levels of publicness.
2. Moderate levels of publicness in the production of either generic or proprietary research products produce a laboratory type which is highly unstable. This instability is the result of high levels of goal conflict within the organization.
3. Higher levels of publicness result in longer-range planning horizons.
4. Proprietary R & D environments result in very short planning horizons and a constant need to "replan" research programs due to market change.
5. Level of publicness is not strongly related to organization structure. Organization structure is largely a function of privateness of market influence. The more generic the R & D product, the more decentralized the structure; and the more proprietary the product, the more centralized the structure.

Implications for Public Policy. Persons interested in developing organization theory for its own sake (surely a small and not very vocal group) should see the value of a conceptualization of publicness-privateness based on the dimensions applied in the foregoing analysis. Others might dismiss the effort as a taxonomic exercise of no importance to the real world of research and development. But there are some significant policy questions that are at least stimulated by the analysis. If one agrees that organization and management issues should play an important role in policy decisions (a tenet of faith in this book), the policy issues take on even greater importance.

The public policy implications of a dimensional approach to the publicness of R & D organization has been explored elsewhere in some detail (Crow and Bozeman, forthcoming-a, forthcoming-b) but should be alluded to here. Four issues are briefly explored.

Direct support of industry R & D. Direct funding of industrial R & D is based on the traditional assumption that government financing of research in industrial labs produces some complementarity between the goals of the firm and those of the government sponsor. It is further assumed that the firm will not invest in research beyond the point at which it is unable to appropriate the returns (in the form of profits to the firm). The foregoing analysis should provide some evidence that industrial firms are actually quite varied and respond to multiple environmental forces. Moreover, increased publicness (that is, greater government funding) is not "firm neutral." It has the potential to affect the structure and performance of the lab and to enhance or increase its effectiveness (Crow and Bozeman, forthcoming-b). A more sophisticated approach to government planning of its support for industrial R & D should permit a less disruptive set of effects on the firm and should permit the matching of R & D support objectives with the characteristics of industrial R & D labs. A dimensional concept of privateness facilitates a more planned approach to direct funding of industrial R & D.

"Privatization" of public R & D labs. In the last several years, there has been increasing interest in greater use of prominent national R & D facilities, all of which receive substantial government funding, for achievement of market goals. Two factors have encouraged the refocusing of public R & D labs: the stagnant economy of the late 1970s and early 1980s and the Reagan administration's broad-based interest in market-oriented public policies. Much of the discussion (and some policy change [see Bozeman and Link, 1983]) has been aimed at the Public Generic labs, especially the so-called national labs of the Department of Energy. The results presented here call into question the wisdom of exerting greater economic pressure on the Public Generics. The

Public Generics are currently quite effective in producing revolutionary technical change and have a unique niche in the population of United States R & D providers. This seems to have been accomplished largely as a result of the government's endowment of political authority, the "sheltering" of the Public Generic from the vicissitudes of the market, and the presence of a stable resource base. The analysis presented here suggests that increased privateness of Public Generics is likely to alter them in several respects, many of which are undesirable from the standpoint of producing high-quality technical change.

Development of cooperative research centers. The National Science Foundation and other groups in the federal government have sought to stimulate the development of industry-university-government research cooperatives. The assumption is that development of such centers will enhance the rate of technical change and permit more rapid assimilation of technical change for economic productivity. The findings presented here suggest that political and market goals lead to predictable conflicts and that these conflicts have important implications for the structure and management of the organization affected. Particularly, the setting of research agendas and the implementation of research plans are more difficult when both political and economic authority exert strong influence. This is not to suggest that research cooperatives are undesirable—only that their structuring must be given considerable forethought. Particularly, it seems desirable to permit decentralization in the setting of the research agenda but to provide stable funding.

R & D tax credits. R & D tax credits are designed to change the internal calculus of the firm in its R & D investment planning. The intent is that the tax credit will provide sufficient stimulus to pursue additional R & D rather than invest in activities that may be in the firm's interest but that provide less social utility.

While tax credits are likely to have some effect on the amount and composition of R & D for Independent Market laboratories, there is not as much reason to believe that they will affect other lab types; moreover, one might argue that the technical change produced by the Independent Market labs has only limited public good characteristics. This may imply that policy makers should provide a range of tax incentives (and other technical change incentives) designed to stimulate additional R & D in a variety of organization types.

Implications for Organizational Effectiveness. There is no better justification for organization theory than enhanced organization effectiveness. One of the major objectives of the NCRL project is improving organization performance and management of R & D organizations. While the findings are presented in detail elsewhere (Crow, 1985; Crow and Bozeman, forthcoming-b), it is worth brief discussion to illustrate how a dimensions of publicness scheme can be employed in the analysis of organization effectiveness.

In the case analysis of thirty-two energy R & D organizations, a number of concepts of organization effectiveness were developed and implemented. A "strategic constituency" assessment queried those persons identified by the labs as "stakeholders" in the labs' R & D activities. These included customers, members of a parent organization, other scientists, government officials, and client groups. A "peer review" assessment was based on evaluations provided by thirty external reviewers (all scientists and engineers) familiar with the laboratories' activities. In a "significant accomplishment" assessment, each lab identified benchmark scientific and technical accomplishments of the past five years, and these were reviewed by at least four external reviewers. Finally, a "qualitative assessment" was performed by the researchers in which the overall effectiveness of each lab was judged in respect to five criteria: funding stability, organization stability, research planning effectiveness, new idea generation, and characteristics of the research climate.

The results indicate that organization effectiveness in the production of generic products increases as government influence increases and effectiveness in the production of market-oriented R & D products increases as economic authority ("privateness") increases. This holds regardless of legal status of the organization. While these findings are not necessarily predictable, they are unsurprising. It has been suggested (Crow and Bozeman, forthcoming-b) that an "alignment" theory of effectiveness is perhaps most appropriate and that contingency variables can be identified which mitigate the impact of authority types on the effectiveness of various laboratory types. Such a theory could be used to predict their effectiveness with respect to a particular set of objectives.

Implications for Public Organization Theory. The analysis presented here has relied on findings of the National Comparative R & D Laboratory Project to illustrate the use and importance of a dimensional publicness framework. But are the findings and approaches more broadly applicable? Certainly R & D organizations present special advantages for implementation of a dimensions of publicness framework: Organizations are greatly varied with respect to environment, structure, and degrees of economic and political authority; organizations' products and activities are identifiable and in many ways comparable.

If a publicness framework seems less appropriate for some sets of organizations (such as insurance companies and government finance offices), a great many other sets of organizations are good candidates for such treatment. Indeed, most of the organizations that have been used in more traditional public-private comparisons seem appropriate subjects for a dimensional approach. Some that come immediately to mind are hospitals, social service agencies, and educational institutions—organizations characterized by sector blurring, privatization attempts, and new organization forms.

It is important to underscore that there are no canonical variables or measures for research application of a dimensional publicness framework. It is not necessary to confine the analysis to measures of government financing or measures of the market impact of products. Political authority has ubiquitous effects, and all that is required for a dimensional analysis of the effect of publicness is that some organizational process is affected by external political authority. Much work remains to be done in the development of useful analytical approaches and measures for a dimensional approach to publicness, but the limit is one of researcher skill and creativity, not one imposed by limits of organizational variation.

8

Implications for Research,
Management Education,
and Effective Management

Every organization theory contains the seeds of a management theory. The most fundamental lesson of the dimensional theory of publicness is radical: Public management is too confining. What is needed is managerial theory and prescription for managing publicness. Public management, in its traditional guise, is set in the context of the government agency. But government agencies are not the only organizations involved in public management. If all organizations are public, then all organizations are involved in managing publicness. If one accepts this much-expanded definition of public management, there are far-reaching implications for management prescription and management education.

The purpose of this concluding chapter is to consider how the development of public organization theory, particularly the piecing together of the publicness puzzle, relates to management effectiveness and to management education. First, however, let us consider possible next developments in public organization theory. What are the possibilities for developing a "paradigm" around the publicness puzzle? How might such a paradigm affect management?

The Publicness Puzzle as "Paradigm"

The dimensional theory of publicness, set out in Chapters Four through Six and applied in Chapter Seven, has some advantages as an analytical framework for public organization theory. The approach is applicable to any organization, helps deal with sector blurring, "privatization," and hybrid organizations, and provides a rudimentary explanation as to why "more public" organizations should differ from "more private" ones. Given the advantages of the publicness framework, is it a good candidate for a public organization administration paradigm? No—not if one means by paradigm "a universally recognized scientific achievement that . . . provides model problems and solutions to a community of [scientific] practitioners" (Kuhn, 1970, p. 11). In this sense of paradigm, public administration has never had a paradigm. Kuhn speaks of the Copernican Revolution and Newtonian physics as paradigms, and by such measures there has never been a paradigm in the social sciences (Ravetz, 1971).

But the term *paradigm* has been used in a great many ways; Kuhn himself seems to use it in more than twenty different ways (Masterman, 1970). If we mean by a paradigm an organizing framework that is highly influential among the researchers in a field (Bozeman, 1979), then public administration has had several paradigms (Henry, 1975). One of the earliest paradigms was scientific management. Early public administration was organized around a set of so-called scientific principles embodied in the writings of Gulick and Urwick (1937) and the father of scientific management, Frederick Taylor (1911). During the scientific management era of public administration, a period roughly spanning the late 1920s to the early 1940s, there was much consensus about its purposes, leading research questions, and even "good management principles." As Simon (1946), Dahl (1947), and others succeeded in overthrowing the orthodoxy of scientific management, a number of competing approaches or "paradigms" emerged. Some of these, such as the administrative sciences paradigm (Simon, 1947) and the public choice paradigm (Ostrom, 1973), have had some longevity, while others, such as the "new public administration" (Marini, 1971), seem to have run their courses. Today's public administration is not paradigmless; instead, it is beset by competing paradigms.

Is the dimensional theory of publicness a suitable candidate for addition to the set of competitors? No. The dimensional theory is not a worthy paradigm candidate because it is only one of several useful approaches to the publicness puzzle. For all its breadth, it is too narrow a definition of publicness. There is, for instance, merit in binary approaches comparing core sets of public administration. At this point, it is useful to retain several approaches to the publicness puzzle. But is the publicness puzzle itself a suitable candidate for a paradigm for public administration? Yes. If we define "paradigm" as a set of core questions guiding research and theory, the publicness puzzle is quite satisfactory as an addition to the competing paradigms of public administration. Indeed, the publicness puzzle is also a sort of paradigm for the practice of public management. It suggests certain approaches to public management and calls attention to managerial strategies and tactics not readily drawn from either a generic or a purely public approach to management.

The Publicness Puzzle as a Paradigm for Research and Theory

The term *publicness puzzle* was chosen with some care. One of Kuhn's (1970) uses of the term *paradigm* is simply as a puzzle that intrigues researchers and theorists. The question of the distinctiveness of public organizations and public management has captured the attention of a great many theorists. And well it should. There is perhaps no question more basic to the study of public management. If the answer to the publicness puzzle is that public organizations and public management are not in any important sense different from generic (or general, or business) approaches, there is really no justification for a separate and identifiable field of scholarship. In that respect, the significance of the publicness puzzle is manifest. But even if one agrees that the publicness puzzle is a suitable organizing framework for research on public organizations and their management, there is more than one beginning point to the solution of the puzzle. Thus, the objective here is to suggest some ways in which sections of the puzzle might be parceled. The focus is on conceptual development.

Conceptual development is a first priority in research on the publicness puzzle, chiefly because much of the research on public organizations proceeds apace with little thought to conceptual development. The result often is a set of empirical findings that is not cumulative, not generalizable, and difficult even to interpret. Research can proceed in the absence of meaningful concepts, but theory cannot. The publicness puzzle does not, of course, suffer from an utter impoverishment of concepts. Beginning with the work of Dahl and Lindblom (1953) and turning later to Wamsley and Zald (1973) and more recently to Benn and Gaus (1983), a variety of useful concepts of publicness has emerged. Furthermore, the old standby—legal status or ownership—used by researchers in the binary tradition remains quite useful. The strategy of identifying "core public" and "core private" organizations and developing theory and research around this less complicated set of organizational actors has much to recommend it. In some respects, this approach is as old as formal organization theory. The archetypes developed by Max Weber are not exactly "core bureaucracies," but the approaches have much in common. Perhaps the key conceptual task for those seeking to further research and theory about core or archetypal public and private organizations is to give further thought as to just what diagnostic characteristics are to be used to designate core public and private. Legal status has some obvious shortcomings.

This book certainly has not preempted conceptual development from the perspective of dimensional approaches to publicness. Much conceptual work remains. Some next steps:

1. Develop publicness measures for a wide variety of organizational activities and processes.
2. Develop concepts closer to actual organization behavior. Concepts such as government financing provide a useful starting point but are not good stand-alone proxies for political authority. Too much is assumed by such a rough approximation.
3. Implement the "decomposition assumption." Chapter Six argues that an organization can be public with respect to some of its activities and not in regard to others. A single measure of publicness obviously does little to advance this notion.
4. Develop concepts that can be applied to a wide variety of organizations with different missions, technologies, and

cultures. At this point, it is useful to "hold constant" organizational product or technology (as in Chapter Seven). As a dimensional theory becomes more powerful, it will be necessary to apply similar concepts and measures in diverse organizational contexts.

Public organization researchers have little history of exploiting theoretical concepts. Conceptual works such as those presented by Wamsley and Zald (1973) and Dahl and Lindblom (1953) seem to influence research, but only indirectly. Researchers are aware of such works, cite them, and use them to develop hypotheses. But rarely do the concepts presented in theoretical works become reworked into constructs used in empirical research. If empirically based theory is to advance, researchers must undertake the challenge of developing useful measures for useful concepts.

The Publicness Puzzle, Public Management,
and Managing Publicness

Public managers can be found in most every type of organization. Public managers include bankers financing urban development loans, bond analysts evaluating municipal bonds, consultants evaluating government programs, defense contractors building the latest fighter jet, and university professors conducting government-sponsored research. In short, public managers are persons who manage publicness. For some of those involved in managing publicness, it is one of many managerial duties and not the most important. For others, almost all their managerial efforts are aimed at managing publicness.

Similar to the binary and generic approaches to organization theory, the practice of public management has been dominated by two perspectives. Many managers feel that there are certain basic principles of good management and that these lead to good results in virtually any context. Others feel that public management requires quite different skills than does business management. But little attention has been given to managing publicness apart from managing government organizations. As discussed in Chapter Two, several features of public management do seem distinctive, including the importance of electoral cycles, the visibility of higher-level public managers, and the stakes involved. However, many of these features also affect business managers engaged in managing publicness.

A reformulation of public management around the notion of managing publicness requires special attention to three issues: (1) the role of the "bottom line" in organization assessment, (2) managing interdependence, and (3) organizational values.

Managing Publicness: "Bottom Line" Management Versus Mixed Motives. One objection to the managing publicness concept is that business managers, even those involved in dealing regularly with political authorities, ultimately look to the "bottom line" to gauge managerial success. According to stereotypes, public management and private management differ fundamentally because public managers don't have to worry about the bottom line. The stereotype (usually close to reality) for the public organization assumes that funding comes from government appropriations. By contrast, the firm's resource acquisition process is much different. It is generally assumed that the firm has much more discretion and control over such factors as development of new products and services, development of new markets, and manipulation of demand for its goods and services. The firm is assumed to have nearly complete autonomy in forming business policy and strategies.

As a result of the character of public-sector financing, the government manager operates without a "bottom line." There is a bottom line in business, and this is often used as the rationale for a sharp demarcation between public and private management. Following these stereotypes, one might conclude that the bottom line of the business manager implies little common ground with the public manager, even if the business manager is involved in managing publicness. However, let us consider what one *cannot* learn from assessments based on profitability measures. In the first place, one cannot determine, except by the most speculative means, the relationship of the firm's profit to its potential profit. Even if its profits go up, it may simply mean that there has been an increase in demand (perhaps unrelated to the activities of the organization) or a change in some other significant external factor. Perhaps a truly effective organization would have realized even greater increases in profit. We can, of course, examine increases in measures of market share, but a decreased market share might simply be explained by the fact that several new firms have entered the market. Likewise, effectiveness measures that consider market share in relation to market concentration are of limited value because the firms often are not comparable. One of many factors that can reduce the comparability of organizations is age: New firms may not yet have begun to benefit fully from economies of scale, and old firms may be disadvantaged by the fact that their equipment and other technology are from an earlier generation; new firms may be disadvantaged by the fact that they cannot exploit certain tax incentives and depreciation allowances, and old firms may be disadvantaged by a natural and even desirable "salary creep."

A second difficulty in the use of profit-related measures of effectiveness is that business firms pursue a multitude of objectives, only some of which can be summarized in profit indicators. Business firms are not interested only in profit but also in such related goals as growth, financial stability, predictability, and less directly related factors, such as innovativeness, control, organizational autonomy, employee job satisfaction, public service, reputation, and competitive advantage. Granted, these factors are sometimes related to profit, but often they are of independent importance. Government and business organizations are characterized by multiple and shifting goals, differential perspectives on the part of stakeholders, limited autonomy, complex interorganizational relations, and limited time horizons.

In sum, the "bottom line" seems not to vitiate the need for a managerial concept based on "managing publicness." In fact, managerial philosophies rooted in bottom line thinking have, according to some observers (Hayes and Abernathy, 1980), victimized American business. As a result of riveting attention to the short-term bottom line, some businesses have imperiled long-term growth, given precedence to "money management" rather than production inputs, and reduced product and process innovation.

Managing publicness assumes that neither the bottom line nor temporal budgetary politics should be the fundamental goal of the manager. A focus on managing publicness assumes that virtually all large organizations have the same underlying motivations and assumptions in their resource acquisition processes. Organizations, including not only business but also government, public service, and not-for-profit organizations, seek stable growth, decision-making autonomy, and control (see Bozeman and Straussman, 1983, for an elaboration of this argument). The mission of the organization is less important than these basic motivations, and these motivations are only minimally affected by the presence or absence of a profit motive. Likewise, one may assume that managing publicness, like other managerial processes, involves the seeking of these core objectives. Managing publicness almost always entails striving for multiple objectives.

Managing Publicness: Interdependence. A recasting of public management to managing publicness entails a focus on interdependence. Typically, an increase in the publicness of an organization leads to an increase in interdependence. Managing interdependence is a special skill and involves attention to factors not so important in organizations with fewer ties to the environment (Whetten and Bozeman, forthcoming). In the first place, managing interdependence generally implies greater complexity. Indeed, complexity is sometimes defined in terms of interdependence (Pfeffer and Salancik, 1978). Secondly, interdependence requires much more attention, and different kinds of attention, to the external environment of the organization. Managers in business firms with low degrees of publicness spend a substantial portion of their time monitoring the environment (Mintzberg, 1972). They must track competitors' performance, look for new markets, and scan the environment for new technological opportunities. But once information is acquired and decisions are made, the implementation of strategy is simplified by the fact that the organization more often acts as a single unit. With high degrees of publicness, environmental monitoring requires much attention to interorganizational partners, as before, but strategy implementation no longer is unitary. Interdependence typically means that organizations act less quickly, decisions have greater impact, and actions are not as easily reversed.

Managing interdependence requires managerial skills not often cultivated in inward-looking or self-directed organizations. One of the most important issues is selection of interorganizational partners whose interests are complementary. Compatibility of mission and compatibility of leadership should both be considered. More difficult yet is compatibility of organization cultures. If two social services agencies link, one oriented toward client service and the other toward field investigation of fraud, each organization's activities can actually weaken those of the other.

Interdependence requires skill at external coordination. Most managers have responsibilities for coordinating units and programs within the organization, but external coordination presents new challenges. For one, the costs (in terms of both time and money) of external coordination are greater. Coordinating external interdependence requires somewhat different skills: persuasion, negotiation, coalition building. In short, political skills take on greater importance in managing interdependence, especially when that interdependence arises from political authority.

Managerial Values. The interdependence created by political authority has implications more fundamental than managerial strategy and technique. The publicness of organizations raises several questions about managerial values: What are the most basic purposes of the manager? What are the ends of the organization? How do the purposes of the manager and the organization match up with the organization's role in society?

Throughout this book, little systematic attention has been paid to organizational or managerial values. In part, this inattention comes from the belief that normative issues have clouded attempts to provide empirically based explanations of differences between public and private organizations. However, any discussion of the implications of publicness for management must give some consideration to the relation between management values and publicness.

According to Mintzberg (1972, p. 95), the "prime function of the manager is to ensure that his organization serves its basic purpose—the efficient production of specific goods or services." But in an organization with a high degree of publicness, this may not be a suitable definition of the manager's role. Whistle blowers reporting cost overruns, misuse of public funds, and inferior technical standards on public projects seem to define their roles in such a way that the organization's interests are subordinate to the whistle blower's concept of the public interest. Of course, most managers are not whistle blowers. (In part, this may be a matter of differences in managerial philosophy and ethics, in part a matter of differences among organizations in the need to blow whistles.) Whistle blowing is still uncommon and sometimes an extreme remedy. The more interesting question is whether publicness does (or should) affect the manager as he or she goes about daily business. As argued in Chapter Two, there is some reason to believe that there is a public service ethic among government employees. Is there, or should there be, a similar ethic among nongovernment managers of publicness?

If we hearken back to the discussion of political authority presented in Chapter Five, it is easy to see why managing publicness might involve a value dimension not present in private management. If the organization is acting on the basis of political authority (endowments or constraints) and the manager is the official embodiment of that authority, then, ultimately, there is a link, however distant, between grants of legitimacy and individual managerial behavior. In some instances, the link is distant enough that it is unlikely to even occur to either the manager or the general public. However, in other instances the link is much closer. Many government contractors, for example, provide goods and services that are vital to the public interest. Defense contractors stand out in this respect. To whom is the manager of a defense contractor responsible? At the extremes, this question poses few difficulties. If the actions of the organization clearly affect the security of the nation, most people would probably agree that the manager's responsibility transcends the organization. But the less dramatic issues are not so easy to resolve. Should the private-sector "publicness manager" worry more about maintaining openness in the firm's decision making? How does this "government in the sunshine" norm stack up against the firm's need to maintain secrecy to keep its competitive advantage? And what about the tradeoff between taxpayer interests and the firm's interest in profits? Once again, this is easily resolved only at the extremes: No one argues that the firms shouldn't make a profit from government contracts; no one argues that firms should be encouraged to engage in illegal acts. But there are gray areas: choices about expense categories to which activities are charged, indirect cost rates (that is, fixed percentage payment for overhead), charging for the time of professional personnel, and so forth. While governments seek legal solutions to such problems, many areas of managerial discretion remain. One of the most formidable challenges of managing publicness is resolution of the tensions between the values accompanying political authority and the organization's market-based objectives.

The Publicness Puzzle and Public Management Education

New paradigms and shifts in paradigms inevitably have strong effects on formal education and training. This is true even with paradigms in the "weak sense": paradigms that are more organizing frameworks than integrating theories. In the case of the publicness puzzle, management education (in both business and public management programs) has outpaced research and theory. Many public management graduate programs continue to uphold the fiction that public and private management are "alike in all unimportant respects" even as they direct their students to business school courses to learn about financial accounting, marketing, or organization behavior. Just as business schools have tacitly recognized the interdependence of economic and political authority through courses on the legal environment of enterprise and government regulation, public management programs have introduced courses on industrial policy, economic development, and business-government relations. Perhaps the best evidence of the changing nature of public management education is the increasing number of public management students entering the "private" sector, many of whom are charged with duties that require a knowledge of the public dimensions of private firms.

Presently, public management education rarely does a good job of equipping public management students to "manage publicness" in the private sector. In part, this may be due to the fact that so many public management educators pass along stereotypes appropriate for traditional public agencies but not relevant to not-for-profit organizations, hybrids, government enterprises, and "high-publicness" businesses. Naturally, public management education cannot be all things to all people, but some self-conscious concern with "managing publicness" (as opposed to traditional public management) would appear beneficial.

But what form might a curriculum geared to managing publicness take? It would not take the form of a generic management program. Generic management programs should provide a student with a good understanding of those tasks and behaviors for which sector context (or publicness-privateness) matters little. In all likelihood, those tasks relate to individual-level behavior based on psychological variables. But for those management behaviors for which the environmental context is everything, a generic approach holds little promise.

A curriculum concerned with managing publicness might look very much like a traditional public management curriculum—but with a twist. Under such an approach, the "uniqueness" of publicness management would not be taken as axiomatic and courses in budgeting, personnel, organization behavior, and such would identify the impacts of political authority (as best they could) and, at the same time, look for generalizable "good practice."

A curriculum is itself a tacit theory. If the curriculum pretends that public management is necessarily unique, it is subject to type B(inary) error; if it assumes that management is management, it is subject to type A(ggregate) error. Public management education, just like public organization theory, must be sensitive to the possibilities for over- and undergeneralization.

The Publicness Puzzle as Taproot for Research,
Education, and Practice

Public management research, education, and practice each have common roots in the publicness puzzle. If one views research and theory as a vital input into education and education as central to the effective practice of public management, the weakness is in research and theory, and much of that weakness pertains to the poor understanding of the publicness puzzle. To be sure, there is no one-to-one correspondence between advances in public organization research and theory and the enhanced effectiveness of public management education and practice. Much of public management is more art than science, as demonstrated by the fact that so many able public managers have little or no formal educational training in public management. But the fact that much of public management success seems not to flow from (current) public management curricula is more challenge than surprise. Public management practice and education rest as much on knowledge from personal experience as on codified knowledge grounded in research and theory. But this simply tells us that one mission of public management research and theory is to explain practice, to find ways to accumulate and formalize the personal knowledge of practitioners.

One route to such knowledge is the publicness puzzle. Students of general and business administration have made progress in blending formal knowledge and personal knowledge. By understanding the distinctive nature of publicness, especially as it affects public management, it may be possible to put public management education and practice on firmer ground. But for now it is the researchers and theorists who need to catch up. It is sensible for harried managers to look for quick solutions and shortcuts. The problem is that public management researchers and theorists have sometimes been just as uncritical of the basic premises upon which their work rests. Sometimes we operate as though the publicness puzzle has been fit together. Such is hardly the case.

References

Adams, B. "The Limits of Muddling Through: Does Anyone in Washington Really Think Anymore?" *Public Administration Review*, 1979, *39* (6), 544-562.

Alchian, A. A. "Private Property and the Relative Cost of Tenure." In P. Bradley (ed.), *The Public Stake in Union Power*. Charlottesville: University of Virginia Press, 1959.

Alchian, A. A. *Some Economics of Property*. Working paper P-2316. Santa Monica, Calif.: Rand Corporation, 1961.

Alchian, A. A. "Some Economics of Property Rights." *Il Politico*, 1965, *3*, 816-829.

Alchian, A. A., and Demsetz, H. "Production, Information Costs, and Economic Organization." *American Economic Review*, 1972, *62*, 777-799.

Alchian, A. A., and Demsetz, H. "The Property Rights Paradigm." *Journal of Economic History*, 1973, *33*, 16-27.

Aldrich, H. "Technology and Organization Structure: A Reexamination of the Findings of the Aston Group." *Administrative Science Quarterly*, 1972, *17*, 26-43.

Aldrich, H. *Organizations and Environments*. Englewood Cliffs, N.J.: Prentice-Hall, 1979.

Aldrich, H., and Herker, D. "Boundary Spanning Roles and Organization Structure." *Academy of Management Review*, Apr. 1977, pp. 217-230.

Allison, G. T., Jr. "Public and Private Management: Are They Fundamentally Alike in All Unimportant Respects?" Paper presented at the Public Management Research Conference, The Brookings Institution, Washington, D.C., November 19-20, 1979.

Anderson, W. *Campaigns: Cases in Political Conflict.* Pacific Palisades, Calif.: Goodyear, 1970.

Appleby, P. H. *Big Democracy.* New York: Knopf, 1945.

Appleby, P. H. "Government Is Different." In D. Waldo (ed.), *Ideas and Issues in Public Administration.* New York: Greenwood, 1953.

Arendt, H. *On Revolution.* New York: Viking Penguin, 1963.

Baas, L. R. "The Constitution as Symbol: The Interpersonal Sources of Meaning of a Secondary Symbol." *American Journal of Political Science,* 1979, *23,* 101–120.

Bellante, D., and Link, A. N. "Are Public Sector Workers More Risk Averse than Private Sector Workers?" *Industrial and Labor Relations Review,* 1981, *34* (3), 408–412.

Benn, S. I., and Gaus, G. F. *Public and Private in Social Life.* New York: St. Martin's Press, 1983.

Bennett, W. L. "Political Sanctification: The Civil Religion and American Politics." *Social Science Information,* 1975, *14* (6), 79–102.

Berle, A. A., and Means, G. C. *The Modern Corporation and Private Property.* New York: Macmillan, 1932.

Bernstein, M. *The Job of the Federal Executive.* Washington, D.C.: The Brookings Institution, 1958.

Black, E. *Politics and the News: The Political Functions of the Mass Media.* Toronto: Butterworth, 1982.

Blau, P., Heydebrand, V., and Stauffer, R. "The Structure of Small Bureaucracies." *American Sociological Review,* 1966, *31,* 179–191.

Blau, P., and Schoenherr, R. *The Structure of Organizations.* New York: Basic Books, 1971.

Blau, P., and Scott, W. R. *Formal Organizations.* San Francisco: Chandler, 1962.

Bluestone, B., Jordan, P., and Sullivan, M. *Aircraft Industry Dynamics.* Boston: Auburn House, 1981.

Blumberg, P. I. "The Politicization of the Corporation." *Business Lawyer,* 1971, *26,* 1551–1587.

Blumenthal, W. M. "Candid Reflections of a Businessman in Washington." In J. L. Perry and K. L. Kraemer (eds.), *Public*

Management: Public and Private Perspectives. Palo Alto, Calif.: Mayfield, 1983.

Bosetzky, H. "Forms of Bureaucratic Organization in Public and Industrial Administration—Trends in the Federal Republic of Germany." *Social Science Information*, 1980, *19* (1), 107-137.

Bower, J. "Effective Public Management." *Harvard Business Review*, 1977, *56*, 129-137.

Bozeman, B. *Public Management and Policy Analysis*. New York: St. Martin's Press, 1979.

Bozeman, B. "Organization Structure and the Effectiveness of Public Agencies." *International Journal of Public Administration*, 1982, *3*, 235-296.

Bozeman, B. "Dimensions of 'Publicness': An Approach to Public Organization Theory." In B. Bozeman and J. Straussman (eds.), *New Directions in Public Administration*. Monterey, Calif.: Brooks/Cole, 1984.

Bozeman, B., and Link, A. N. *Investments in Technology: Corporate Strategies and Public Policy Alternatives*. New York: Praeger, 1983.

Bozeman, B. L., and Loveless, S. "Sector Context and Performance: A Comparison of Industrial and Government Research Units." *Administration and Society*, forthcoming.

Bozeman, B. L., and Straussman, J. "Organization 'Publicness' and Resource Processes." In R. Hall and R. E. Quinn (eds.), *Organization Theory and Public Policy*. Newbury Park, Calif.: Sage, 1983.

Breton, A., and Winetrobe, R. *The Logic of Bureaucratic Conduct: An Economic Analysis of Competition, Exchange, and Efficiency in Private and Public Organizations*. Cambridge, England: Cambridge University Press, 1982.

Bruggink, T. H. "Public Versus Regulated Private Enterprise in the Municipal Water Industry: A Comparison of Operating Costs." *Quarterly Review of Economics and Business*, 1982, *22*, 111-125.

Buchanan, B. "Government Managers, Business Executives and Organizational Commitment." *Public Administration Review*, 1974, *34* (4), 339-347.

Buchanan, B. "Red-Tape and the Service Ethic: Some Unexpected Differences Between Public and Private Managers." *Administration and Society*, 1975a, *6* (4), 423–438.

Buchanan, B. "To Walk an Extra Mile: The Whats, Whens and Whys of Organizational Commitment." *Organizational Dynamics*, 1975b, *4*, 67–80.

Buchanan, J. *The Demand and Supply of Public Goods*. Skokie, Ill.: Rand McNally, 1973.

Califano, J. *Governing America: An Insider's Report from the White House and the Cabinet*. New York: Simon & Schuster, 1981.

Cameron, K. S. "Critical Questions in Assessing Organizational Effectiveness." *Organization Dynamics*, 1980, *9*, 66–80.

Cameron, K. S., and Whetten, D. A. "Perceptions of Organizational Effectiveness over Organizational Life-Cycles." *Administrative Science Quarterly*, 1981, *26* (4), 525–544.

Campbell, A. "Civil Service Reform." *Public Administration Review*, 1978, *38* (2), 99–103.

Capon, N. "Marketing Strategy Differences Between State and Privately Owned Corporations." *Journal of Marketing*, 1981, *45* (2), 11–18.

Casstevens, T. W. "Birth and Death Processes of Government Bureaus in the United States." *Behavioral Science*, 1980, *25* (2), 161–165.

Cathcart, P. *The Media and Government Leaks*. Washington, D.C.: Standing Committee on Law and National Security, American Bar Association, 1984.

Cayer, N. J. *Public Personnel Administration in the United States*. New York: St. Martin's Press, 1977.

Cheung, S. "Transactions Costs, Risk Aversion and Contractual Arrangements." *Journal of Law and Economics*, 1969, *12*, 23–42.

Child, J. "Strategies of Control and Organization Behavior." *Administrative Science Quarterly*, 1973, *18*, 1–17.

Clarkson, K. W. "Some Implications of Property Rights in Hospital Management." *Journal of Law and Economics*, 1972, *12*, 363–384.

Clarkson, K. W. "Managerial Behavior in Nonproprietary Organizations." In K. W. Clarkson and D. L. Martin (eds.), *The Economics of Nonproprietary Organizations*. Greenwich, Conn.: JAI Press, 1980.

Cleveland, R., and Graham, F. (eds.). *The Aviation Annual of 1946*. New York: Doubleday, 1946.

Cobb, R., and Elder, C. "The Political Uses of Symbolism." *American Politics Quarterly*, 1973, *1*, 305–338.

Cochran, C. E. "Authority and Community." *American Political Science Review*, 1977, *71*, 546–558.

Committee for Economic Development. *Public-Private Partnership: An Opportunity for Urban Communities*. Washington, D.C.: Committee for Economic Development, 1982.

Crow, M. *The Effect of Publicness on Organizational Performance: A Comparative Study of R & D Laboratories*. National Technical Information Service No. PB85–216646. Springfield, Va.: National Technical Information Service, 1985.

Crow, M., and Bozeman, B. "The Evolution of R & D Laboratories: Implications for Policy Analysis." *Journal of Policy Analysis and Management*, forthcoming-a.

Crow M., and Bozeman, B. "R & D Laboratories' Environmental Contexts: Are the Government Lab–Industrial Lab Stereotypes Still Valid?" *Research Policy*, forthcoming-b.

Cunningham, W. G. *The Aircraft Industry*. Los Angeles: Morrison, 1951.

Dahl, R. A. "The Science of Public Administration: Three Problems." *Public Administration Review*, 1947, *7*, 1–11.

Dahl, R. A. *A Preface to Democratic Theory*. Chicago: University of Chicago Press, 1956.

Dahl, R. A., and Lindblom, C. E. *Politics, Economics and Welfare*. New York: Harper & Row, 1953.

Dalton, D. R., and others. "Organization Structure and Performance: A Critical Review." *Academy of Management Review*, 1980, *5*, 49–64.

Davies, D. G. "The Efficiency of Public Vs. Private Firms: The Case of Australia's Two Airlines." *Journal of Law and Economics*, 1971, *14*, 149–165.

Davies, D. G. "Property Rights and Economic Efficiency: The Australian Airlines Revisited." *Journal of Law and Economics,* 1977, *20,* 223-226.

Davies, D. G. "Property Rights and Economic Behavior in Private and Government Enterprises: The Case of Australia's Banking System." In R. O. Zerbe, Jr. (ed.), *Research in Law and Economics.* Vol. 3. Greenwich, Conn.: JAI Press, 1981.

De Alessi, L. "Implications of Property Rights for Government Investment Choices." *American Economic Review,* 1969, *59,* 13-24.

De Alessi, L. "Private Property and Dispersion of Ownership in Large Corporations." *Journal of Finance,* 1973, *28,* 839-851.

De Alessi, L. "The Economics of Property Rights: A Review of the Evidence." In R. O. Zerbe, Jr. (ed.), *Research in Law and Economics.* Vol 2. Greenwich, Conn.: JAI Press, 1980.

Demac, D. *Keeping America Uninformed: Government Secrecy in the 1980's.* New York: Pilgrim Press, 1984.

Demsetz, H. "Some Aspects of Property Rights." *Journal of Law and Economics,* 1966, *9,* 61-70.

Demsetz, H. "Toward a Theory of Property Rights." *American Economic Review,* 1967, *57,* 347-359.

Desai, U., and Crow, M. M. "Failures of Power and Intelligence." *Administration and Society,* 1983, *15* (2), 185-206.

Di Lorenzo, T. J., and Robinson, R. "Managerial Objectives Subject to Political Market Constraints: Electrical Utilities in the United States." *Quarterly Review of Economics and Business,* 1982, *22,* 113-125.

Downs, A. *Inside Bureaucracy.* Boston: Little, Brown, 1967.

Drucker, P. "Managing the Public Service Institution." *The Public Interest,* 1973, *33* (1), 43-46.

Dupree, A. H. *Science in the Federal Government: A History of Policies and Activities to 1940.* Cambridge, Mass.: Harvard University Press, 1957.

Durant, R. F. "From Complacence to Compliance: Toward a Theory of Intragovernmental Regulation." *Administration and Society,* 1986, *17* (4), 433-459.

Dutton, W., and Kraemer, K. "Technology and Urban Management:

The Power Payoffs of Computing." *Administration and Society,* 1977, *9* (3), 305-340.

Dye, T. R., and Pickering, J. W. "Government and Corporate Elites: Convergence and Divergence." *Journal of Politics,* 1974, *36* (4), 900-925.

Eccles, R. G. "Bureaucratic Versus Craft Administration: The Relationship of Market Structure to the Construction Firm." *Administrative Science Quarterly,* 1981, *26* (3), 449-469.

Edelman, M. *The Symbolic Uses of Politics.* Urbana: University of Illinois Press, 1964.

Edmunds, S. W. *Basics of Private and Public Management.* Lexington, Mass.: D.C. Heath, 1978.

Eells, R. *The Government of Corporations.* New York: Free Press, 1962.

Emery, F. E., and Trist, E. L. "The Causal Texture of Organizational Environments." *Human Relations,* 1965, *18,* 21-32.

Emmert, M., and Crow, M. "Public, Private and Hybrid Organizations: An Empirical Examination of the Role of Publicness." *Administration and Society,* forthcoming.

Etzioni, A. *Modern Organizations.* Englewood Cliffs, N.J.: Prentice-Hall, 1977.

Fiedler, F., and Gillo, M. "Correlates of Performance in Community Colleges." *Journal of Higher Education,* 1974, *45,* 672-681.

Finney, G. "Public-Private Partnerships." Paper presented at the National Academy of Public Administration Conference on Government's Use of Non-Profit Agencies to Manage Social Research, Washington, D.C., November 1978.

Fitch, L. C. "Increasing the Role of the Private Sector in Providing Public Services." In W. D. Hawley and D. Rogers (eds.), *Improving the Quality of Urban Management.* Newbury Park, Calif.: Sage, 1974.

Fottler, M. D. "Is Management Really Generic?" *Academy of Management Review,* 1981, *6* (1), 1-12.

Fottler, M. D., and Townsend, N. A. "Characteristics of Public and Private Personnel Directors." *Public Personnel Management,* 1977, *6* (3), 250-258.

Fowlkes, F. "Foes of Lockheed Loan Guarantee Challenge Basic

Premises Behind Proposal." *National Journal,* May 24, 1971, pp. 1151-1155.

Frankel, C. "Political Disobedience and the Denial of Political Authority." *Social Theory and Practice,* 1972, *2* (1), 85-98.

Fraser, J. "Validating a Measure of National Political Legitimacy." *American Journal of Political Science,* 1974, *18,* 117-134.

Frech, H. E. "Health Insurance: Private, Mutuals, or Government." In R. O. Zerbe (ed.), *Research in Law and Economics.* Vol. 2. Greenwich, Conn.: JAI Press, 1980.

Freeman, J. H. "The Unit of Analysis in Organizational Research." In M. W. Meyer and Associates, *Environments and Organizations: Theoretical and Empirical Perspectives.* San Francisco: Jossey-Bass, 1978.

Friedman, M. *Politics and Tyranny: Lessons in the Pursuit of Freedom.* San Francisco: Pacific Institute for Public Policy Research, 1984.

Friedrich, C. *Man and His Government.* New York: McGraw-Hill, 1963.

Fusfeld, H., and Langlois, R. *Understanding R & D Productivity.* Elmsford, N. Y.: Pergamon Press, 1982.

Galbraith, J. *The New Industrial State.* Boston: Houghton Mifflin, 1967.

Goodsell, C. T. "Bureaucratic Manipulation of Physical Symbols: An Empirical Study." *American Journal of Political Science,* 1977, *21,* 79-91.

Goodsell, C. T. *The Case of Bureaucracy.* Chatham, N.J.: Chatham House, 1983.

Grady, R. "Obligation, Consent, and Locke's Right to Revolution: Who Is to Judge?" *Canadian Journal of Political Science,* 1976, *9* (2), 277-292.

Grafstein, R. "The Legitimacy of Political Institutions." *Polity,* 1981, *14* (1), 51-69.

Graham, G. J. *Methodological Foundations for Political Analysis.* Waltham, Mass.: Xerox College, 1971.

Greenstein, F. "The Benevolent Leader: Children's Images of Political Authority." *American Political Science Review,* 1960, *54* (4), 934-943.

Grupp, F. W., and Richard, A. R. "Job Satisfaction Among State Executives in the U.S." *Public Personnel Management,* 1975, *4,* 104-109.

Gulick, L., and Urwick, L. (eds.). *Papers on the Science of Administration.* New York: Institute of Public Administration, 1937.

Gusfield, J. R. *The Culture of Public Problems.* Chicago: University of Chicago Press, 1981.

Guyot, J. F. "Government Bureaucrats Are Different." *Public Administration Review,* 1962, *20* (3), 195-202.

Haga, W. J. "Managerial Professionalism and the Use of Organization Resources." *American Journal of Economics and Sociology,* 1976, *35* (4), 337-348.

Hall, R. *Organizations: Structure and Process.* (2nd ed.) Englewood Cliffs, N.J.: Prentice-Hall, 1977.

Hall, R., Haas, J., and Johnson, N. "Organization Size, Complexity, and Formalism." *American Sociological Review,* 1967, *36* (6), 903-912.

Hall, R., and Quinn, R. E. (eds.). *Organization Theory and Public Policy.* Newbury Park, Calif.: Sage, 1983.

Hannigan, J. A., and Kueneman, R. M. "Legitimacy and Public Organization." *Canadian Journal of Sociology,* 1977, *2* (1), 125-135.

Hayes, F. O. "Innovation in State and Local Government." In F. D. Hayes and J. E. Rasmussen (eds.), *Centers for Innovation in the Cities and States.* San Francisco: San Francisco Press, 1972.

Hayes, R., and Abernathy, W. "Managing Our Way to Economic Decline." *Harvard Business Review,* 1980, *58,* 67-77.

Henry, N. "Paradigms of Public Administration." *Public Administration Review,* 1975, *35,* 378-386.

Herber, B. *Modern Public Finance.* (Rev. ed.) Homewood, Ill.: Irwin, 1971.

Herbst, P. G. "Measurement of Structure by Means of Input-Output Data." *Human Relations,* 1957, *10,* 335-346.

Hess, R. "The Socialization of Attitudes Toward Political Authority." *International Social Science Journal,* 1963, *15* (4), 542-559.

Hibbs, D. A. "Reagan Mandate from the 1980 Elections: A Shift to the Right." *American Politics Quarterly,* 1982, *10* (4), 387-420.

Hoenack, S. A. *Economic Behavior Within Organizations.*
Cambridge, England: Cambridge University Press, 1983.

Holdaway, E., Newberry, J. F., Hickson, D. J., and Heron, R. P.
"Dimensions of Organizations in Complex Societies: The
Educational Sector." *Administrative Science Quarterly,* 1975, *20,*
37-58.

Holden, T. "An Analysis of the Role of Publicness in Political
Science." Paper presented at annual meeting of the American
Political Science Association, Washington, D.C., August 1986.

Holmes, R. *Legitimacy and the Politics of the Knowable.* Boston:
Routledge & Kegan Paul, 1976.

Hood, C., and Dunsire, A. *Bureaumetrics: The Quantitative
Comparison of British Central Government Agencies.* University: University of Alabama Press, 1981.

Horwitch, M. "Designing and Managing Large Scale Public-
Private Technological Enterprises: A State of the Art Review."
Technology in Society, 1979, *1* (3), 179-192.

Horwitch, M., and Prahalad, C. "Managing Multi-Organizational
Enterprises." *Sloan Management Review,* 1981, *2,* 3-16.

James, D. R., and Soref, M. "Profit Constraints on Managerial
Autonomy." *American Sociological Review,* 1981, *46* (1), 1-18.

Jensen, M. C., and Meckling, W. H. "Theory of the Firm,
Managerial Behavior, Agency Costs and Ownership Structure."
Journal of Financial Economics, 1976, *3,* 305-360.

Kann, M. E. "The Dialectic of Consent Theory." *Journal of
Politics,* 1978, *40,* 386-408.

Katz, D., and Kahn, R. *The Social Psychology of Organizations.*
(2nd ed.) New York: Wiley, 1978.

Kaufman, H. "Emerging Conflicts in the Doctrines of Public
Administration." *Public Administration Review,* 1956, *50,*
1057-1073.

Kaufman, H. *Are Government Organizations Immortal?* Washington, D.C.: The Brookings Institution, 1976.

Kaufman, H. *The Administrative Behavior of Federal Bureau
Chiefs.* Washington, D.C.: The Brookings Institution, 1981.

Kaufman, H. *Time, Chance and Organizations.* Chatham, N.J.:
Chatham House, 1985.

Kelsen, H. *General Theory of Law and State.* Cambridge, Mass.: Harvard University Press, 1949.

Kilpatrick, F. P., Cummings, M. C., Jr., and Jennings, M. K. *The Image of the Federal Service.* Washington, D.C.: The Brookings Institution, 1964.

Kimberly, J. "Issues in the Design of Longitudinal Organizational Research." *Administrative Science Quarterly,* 1976a, *4* (3), 321-347.

Kimberly, J. "Organization Size and the Structuralist Perspective." *Administrative Science Quarterly,* 1976b, *21,* 571-597.

Kimberly, J. R., Miles, R. H., and Associates. *The Organizational Life Cycle: Issues in the Creation, Transformation, and Decline of Organizations.* San Francisco: Jossey-Bass, 1980.

Kogod, R. P., and Caulfield, S. C. "Beyond Corporate Responsibility: Toward a Fundamental Redefinition of the Roles of Public and Private Sectors." *National Journal,* 1982, *22,* 981-985.

Kotler, P. E., and Sidney, J. L. "Broadening the Concept of Marketing." *Journal of Marketing,* 1969, *33* (1), 10-15.

Kourvetaris, G., and Dobratz, B. A. "Political Power and Conventional Political Participation." *Annual Review of Sociology,* 1982, *8,* 289-317.

Kuhn, T. *The Structure of Scientific Revolutions.* (2nd ed.) Chicago: University of Chicago Press, 1970.

Lau, A. W., Newman, A. R., and Broedling, L. A. "The Nature of Managerial Work in the Public Sector." *Public Administration Review,* 1980, *40,* 513-520.

Lee, B. (ed.). *Aviation Facts and Figures, 1957.* New York: McGraw-Hill, 1957.

Lerner, A. W. "Ambiguity and Organizational Analysis: The Consequences of Micro Versus Macro Conceptualization." *Administration and Society,* 1986, *17* (4), 461-480.

Levenson, A. B. *Government Information: Freedom of Information Act, Sunshine Act, Privacy Act.* New York: Practising Law Institute, 1978.

Levine, C. "The Federal Government in the Year 2000: Administrative Legacies of the Reagan Administration." *Public Administration Review,* 1986, *46* (3), 195-206.

Lindblom, C. E. *Politics and Markets*. New York: Basic Books, 1977.

Lindsay, C. M. "A Theory of Government Enterprise." *Journal of Political Economy*, 1976, *84*, 1061–1078.

Lipset, S. *Political Man*. New York: Doubleday, 1963.

Loveless, S. *Sector Status, Structure and Performance: A Comparison of Public and Private Research Units*. Unpublished doctoral dissertation, Syracuse University, 1985.

Lovich, N. P., Shaffer, P. L., Hopkins, R. H., and Yale, D. A. "Do Public Servants Welcome or Fear Merit Evaluation of Their Performance?" *Public Administration Review*, 1980, *40* (3), 214–221.

Lowery, D., and Rusbult, C. E. "Bureaucratic Responses to Antibureaucratic Administrations: Federal Employee Reaction to the Reagan Election." *Administration and Society*, 1986, *18* (1), 45–76.

Lowi, T. J. *The End of Liberalism*. New York: Norton, 1969.

Lynn, L. E. *Managing the Public's Business*. New York: Basic Books, 1981.

Lynn, N., and Vaden, R. E. "Federal Executives: Initial Reactions to Change." *Administration and Society*, 1980, *1* (12), 101–120.

McKelvey, B. *Organizational Systematics*. Berkeley: University of California Press, 1982.

McWilliams, W. C. "On Political Illegitimacy." *Public Policy*, 1971, *29*, 440–454.

Mahoney, T., Frost, P., Crandall, N., and Weitzel, W. "The Conditioning Influence of Organizations' Size Upon Managerial Practice." *Organization Behavior and Human Performance*, 1972, *8*, 230–241.

Mainzer, L. C. *Political Bureaucracy*. Glenview, Ill.: Scott, Foresman, 1973.

Malek, F. V. "Mr. Executive Goes to Washington." *Harvard Business Review*, 1972, *50*, 63–68.

Marcson, S. *The Scientist in American Industry*. New York: Harper & Row, 1960.

Marcson, S. "Research Settings." In S. Nagi and R. Corwin (eds.), *The Social Contexts of Research*. New York: Wiley-Interscience, 1972.

Marini, F. (ed.). *Toward a New Public Administration.* Scranton, Pa.: Chandler, 1971.

Martin, R. "Two Models for Justifying Political Authority." *Ethics,* 1975, *86,* 1, 70–75.

Masterman, M. "The Nature of a Paradigm." In I. Lakatos and A. Musgrave (eds.), *Criticism and the Growth of Knowledge.* Cambridge, England: Cambridge University Press, 1970.

Mazzolini, R. "European Government Controlled Enterprises: Explaining International Strategies and Policy Decisions." *Journal of Business Studies,* 1979, *10* (3), 16–27.

Merelman, R. M. "Learning and Legitimacy." *American Political Science Review,* 1966, *60,* 548–567.

Methe, D., Baesel, J., and Schulman, S. "Applying Principles of Corporate Finance in the Public Sector." In J. L. Perry and K. L. Kraemer (eds.), *Public Management: Public and Private Perspectives.* Palo Alto, Calif.: Mayfield, 1983.

Meyer, J. W., and Rowan, B. "Institutionalized Organizations: Formal Structure Versus Myth and Ceremony." *American Journal of Sociology,* 1977, *83* (2), 340–363.

Meyer, M. W. *Bureaucratic Structure and Authority: Coordination and Control in 254 Government Agencies.* New York: Harper & Row, 1972.

Meyer, M. W. *Change in Public Bureaucracies.* Cambridge, England: Cambridge University Press, 1979.

Meyer, M. W. "'Bureaucratic' Versus 'Profit' Organization." In B. Staw and L. L. Cummings (eds.), *Research in Organizational Behavior.* Greenwich, Conn.: JAI Press, 1982.

Meyer, M. W., Marshall, W., and Williams, R. O. *Comparison of Innovation in Public and Private Sectors: An Exploratory Study.* Washington, D.C.: Division of Policy Research and Analysis, National Science Foundation, 1977.

Miles, R. *Macro Organization Behavior.* Glenview, Ill.: Scott, Foresman, 1980.

Mintzberg, H. *The Nature of Managerial Work.* New York: Harper & Row, 1972.

Mitnick, B. *The Political Economy of Regulation.* New York: Columbia University Press, 1979.

Moe, T. "The Economics of Organization." *American Journal of Political Science,* 1984, *28,* 739-777.

Mohr, L. B. "The Concept of Organizational Goals." *American Political Science Review,* 1973, *67,* 469-484.

Mohr, L. B. *Explaining Organizational Behavior: The Limits and Possibilities of Theory and Research.* San Francisco: Jossey-Bass, 1982.

Morgan, R. J. "Madison's Analysis of the Sources of Political Authority." *American Political Science Review,* 1981, *75,* 613-625.

Mosher, F. C. *The GAO: The Quest for Accountability in American Government.* Boulder, Colo.: Westview Press, 1979.

Mowery, D. *The Emergence and Growth of Industrial Research in American Manufacturing, 1899-1945.* Unpublished doctoral dissertation, Stanford University, 1981.

Murray, M. A. "Comparing Public and Private Management: An Exploratory Essay." *Public Administration Review,* 1975, *34* (4), 364-371.

Musolf, L. *Uncle Sam's Private Profitseeking Corporations: Comsat, Fannie Mae, Amtrack, and Conrail.* Lexington, Mass.: Lexington Books, 1983.

Musolf, L., and Seidman, H. "The Blurred Boundaries of Public Administration." *Public Administration Review,* 1980, *40,* 124-130.

National Center for Productivity and Quality of Working Life. *Employee Attitudes and Productivity: Differences Between the Public and Private Sector.* Washington, D.C.: United States Civil Service Commission, 1978.

Neuberg, L. G. "Two Issues in the Municipal Ownership of Electric Power Distribution Systems." *Bell Journal of Economics,* 1977, *18,* 303-323.

Niskanen, W. A. *Bureaucracy and Representative Government.* Hawthorne, N.Y.: Aldine, 1971.

Nystrom, P. C., and Starbuck, W. H. (eds.). *Handbook of Organizational Design.* New York: Oxford University Press, 1981.

Olsen, J. B. "Applying Business Management Skills to Governmental Operations." *Public Administration Review,* 1979, *39* (3), 282-289.

Ostrom, V. *The Intellectual Crisis in Public Administration.* University: University of Alabama Press, 1973.

Ouchi, W. G. "Markets, Bureaucracies and Clans." *Administrative Science Quarterly*, 1980, *25* (1), 129-141.

Padgett, L. *The Mexican Political System.* Boston: Houghton Mifflin, 1966.

Palmer, J., and Sawhill, I. *The Reagan Experiment: An Examination of Economic and Social Policies Under the Reagan Administration.* Washington, D.C.: Urban Institute Press, 1982.

Pearce, J. L., and Perry, J. L. "Federal Merit Pay: A Longitudinal Analysis." *Public Administration Review*, 1983, *43* (4), 315-325.

Peltzman, S. "Pricing in Public and Private Enterprises: Electric Utilities in the United States." *Journal of Law and Economics*, 1971, *14*, 109-148.

Perry, J. L., and Kraemer, K. L. (eds.). *Public Management: Public and Private Perspectives.* Palo Alto, Calif.: Mayfield, 1983.

Perry, J. L., and Porter, L. W. "Factors Affecting the Context for Motivation in Public Organizations." *Academy of Management Review*, 1982, *7*, 89-98.

Pfeffer, J. "Administrative Regulation and Licensing: Social Problem or Solution?" *Social Problems*, 1974, *17*, 218-228.

Pfeffer, J., and Leong, A. "Resource Allocations in United Funds: Examination of Power and Dependence." *Social Forces*, 1977, *55* (3), 775-790.

Pfeffer, J., and Salancik, G. *The External Control of Organizations.* New York: Harper & Row, 1978.

Pinder, C. C., and Moore, L. F. "The Resurrection of Taxonomy to Aid the Development of Middle-Range Theories of Organizational Behavior." *Administrative Science Quarterly*, 1979, *24*, 99-118.

Ponzer, B. Z., and Schmidt, W. W. "Determining Managerial Strategies in the Public Sector: What Kind of People Enter the Public and Private Sectors?" *Human Resource Management*, 1982, *18* (1), 35-43.

Pool, I. *Symbols of Democracy.* Stanford, Calif.: Stanford University Press, 1952.

Porter, L. W., and Perry, J. L. "Motivation and Public Management: Concepts and Issues." Paper presented at the Public Management Research Conference, The Brookings Institution, Washington, D.C., November 19-20, 1979.

Provan, K., Beyer, J. M., and Kruybosch, C. "Environmental Linkages and Power in Resource-Dependence Relations Between Organizations." *Administrative Science Quarterly,* 1980, *25* (2), 200-225.

Pugh, D. S., Hickson, D. J., and Hinings, C. R. "The Context of Organization Structures." *Administrative Science Quarterly,* 1969, *14,* 91-114.

Pugh, D. S., Hickson, D. J., Hinings, C. R., and Turner, C. "Dimensions of Organization Structure." *Administrative Science Quarterly,* 1968, *13* (1), 65-91.

Rainey, H. G. "Perceptions of Incentives in Business and Government: Implications for Civil Service Reform." *Public Administration Review,* 1979, *39* (5), 440-448.

Rainey, H. G. "Public Agencies and Private Firms: Incentives, Goals, and Individual Roles." *Administration and Society,* 1983, *15* (2), 207-242.

Rainey, H. G., Backoff, R. W., and Levine, C. H. "Comparing Public and Private Organizations." *Public Administration Review,* 1976, *36* (2), 233-246.

Ravetz, J. *Scientific Knowledge and Its Social Problems.* New York: Oxford University Press, 1971.

Rawls, J. *A Theory of Justice.* Cambridge, Mass.: Harvard University Press, 1971.

Rawls, J. R., Ullrich, R. A., and Nelson, O. T. "A Comparison of Managers Entering or Re-entering the Profit and Nonprofit Sectors." *Academy of Management Journal,* 1975, *18* (4), 616-622.

Redford, E. "Business as Government." In R. Martin (ed.), *Public Administration and Democracy: Essays in Honor of Paul H. Appleby.* Syracuse, N.Y.: Syracuse University Press, 1965.

Reimann, B. C., and Neghandhi, A. R. "Organization Structure and Effectiveness." In R. H. Kilmann, L. R. Pondy, and D. P. Slevin (eds.), *The Management of Organization Design.* Amsterdam: North Holland, 1976.

Revans, R. W. "Human Relations, Management, and Size." In F. M. Hugh-Jones (ed.), *Human Relations and Modern Management.* Amsterdam: North Holland, 1958.

Rhinehart, J. B., and others. "Comparative Study of Need Satisfaction in Governmental and Business Hierarchies." *Journal of Applied Psychology,* 1969, *53* (3), 230–235.

Rice, B. *The C-5A Scandal.* Boston: Houghton Mifflin, 1971.

Ring, P. S., and Perry, J. L. "Reforming the Upper Levels of Bureaucracy: A Longitudinal Study of the Senior Executive Service." *Administration and Society,* 1983, *15* (1), 119–144.

Roberts, K. H., Hulin, C. L., and Rousseau, D. M. *Developing an Interdisciplinary Science of Organizations.* San Francisco: Jossey-Bass, 1978.

Roessner, J. D. "Incentives to Innovate in Public and Private Organizations: Implications for Public Policy." *Administration and Society,* 1977, *9*, 341–365.

Rose, R. "Implementation and Evaporation: The Record of MBO." *Public Administration Review,* 1977, *27* (1), 64–71.

Rosen, B. "Crises in the U.S. Civil Service." *Public Administration Review,* 1986, *46* (3), 207–214.

Rothschild, J. "Observation on Political Legitimacy in Contemporary Europe." *Political Science Quarterly,* 1977, *92*, 487–501.

Rowan, B. "Organizational Structure and the Institutional Environment: The Case of Public Schools." *Administrative Science Quarterly,* 1982, *27*, 259–279.

Roy, W. G. "The Process of Bureaucratization in the United States State Department and the Vesting of Economic Interests, 1886–1905." *Administrative Science Quarterly,* 1981, *26* (3), 419–433.

Rumsfeld, D. "A Politician Turned Executive." *Fortune,* 1979, *100*, 88–94.

Runciman, W. G. *Social Science and Political Theory.* Cambridge, England: Cambridge University Press, 1963.

Rushing, W. "Differences in Profit and Nonprofit Hospitals: A Study of Effectiveness and Efficiency in General Short-Stay Hospitals." *Administrative Science Quarterly,* 1973, *18*, 474–484.

Rushing, W. "Profit and Nonprofit Orientations and the Differentiation-Coordination Hypothesis for Organizations: A Study of Small General Hospitals." *American Sociological Review,* 1976, *41*, 676–691.

Samuelson, P. *The Collected Scientific Papers of Paul A. Samuelson.* Cambridge, Mass.: MIT Press, 1966.

Savas, E. S. *Privatizing the Public Sector.* Chatham, N.J.: Chatham House, 1982.

Schaar, J. H. "Legitimacy in the Modern State." In P. Green and S. Levinson (eds.), *Power and Community.* New York: Vintage Books, 1970.

Schiesl, M. H. *The Politics of Efficiency: Municipal Administration and Reform in America, 1800-1920.* Berkeley: University of California Press, 1977.

Schmidt, R. E., and Abramson, M. A. "Politics and Performance: What Does It Mean for Civil Servants?" *Public Administration Review,* 1983, *43* (2), 155-160.

Segal, M. "Organization and Environment: A Typology." *Public Administration Review,* 1974, *34,* 212-219.

Seidman, H. "Government-Sponsored Enterprise in the United States." In B. Smith (ed.), *The New Political Economy: The Public Use of the Private Sector.* New York: Wiley, 1975.

Selznick, P. *TVA and the Grass Roots.* New York: Harper & Row, 1966.

Sharkansky, I. *Routines of Politics.* New York: Van Nostrand Reinhold, 1970.

Shaw, L. C., and Clark, R. T., Jr. "The Practical Differences Between Public and Private Sector Collective Bargaining." *UCLA Law Review,* 1972, *19,* 867-886.

Shelton, J. "Allocative Efficiency v. 'X-Efficiency': Comment." *American Economic Review,* 1967, *57,* 1252-1258.

Shubert, G. "The Public Interest in Administrative Decision-Making: Theorem, Theosophy or Theory." *American Political Science Review,* 1957, *51,* 346-368.

Simon, H. "The Proverbs of Administration." *Public Administration Review,* 1946, *6,* 53-67.

Simon, H. *Administrative Behavior.* New York: Free Press, 1947.

Simonson, G. R. *The History of the American Aircraft Industry.* Cambridge, Mass.: MIT Press, 1968.

Smart, C., and Vertinsky, I. "Designs for Crisis Decision Units." *Administrative Science Quarterly,* 1977, *22,* 640-657.

Smith, S. P. "Prospects for Reforming Federal Pay." *American Economic Review,* 1982, *72* (2), 273-277.

Steckler, H. *The Structure and Performance of the Aerospace Industry.* Berkeley: University of California Press, 1965.

Stillman, P. "The Concept of Legitimacy." *Polity,* 1974, 7 (1), 33–56.

Straussman, J. D. "More Bang for Fewer Bucks? Or How Local Governments Can Rediscover the Potentials (and Pitfalls) of the Market." *Public Administration Review,* 1981, *41,* 150–157.

Taylor, F. *Principles of Scientific Management.* New York: Harper & Row, 1911.

Thompson, J. *Organizations in Action.* New York: McGraw-Hill, 1967.

Thompson, V. *Modern Organizations.* New York: Knopf, 1964.

Tolbert, P. S., and Zucker, L. G. "Institutional Sources of Change in the Formal Structure of Organizations: The Diffusion of Civil Service Reform, 1880–1935." *Administrative Science Quarterly,* 1983, *28,* 22–39.

Tussman, J. *Obligation and the Body Politic.* New York: Oxford University Press, 1960.

U.S. Office of Personnel Management. *Federal Employee Attitudes.* Washington, D.C.: U.S. Office of Personnel Management, 1979.

Vogel, D. "The Corporation as Government." *Polity,* 1975, *8,* 5–37.

Walsh, A. H. *The Public's Business: The Politics and Practices of Government Corporations.* Cambridge, Mass.: MIT Press, 1978.

Wamsley, G. L., and Zald, M. N. *The Political Economy of Public Organizations.* Lexington, Mass.: D.C. Heath, 1973.

Warwick, D. P. *A Theory of Public Bureaucracy.* Cambridge, Mass.: Harvard University Press, 1975.

Weber, M. *The Theory of Economic and Social Organization.* New York: Free Press, 1947.

Weick, K. *The Social Psychology of Organizing.* Reading, Mass.: Addison-Wesley, 1969.

Weissberg, R. "Adolescents' Perceptions of Political Authorities: Another Look at Political Virtue and Power." *Midwest Journal of Political Science,* 1972, *16* (1), 147–168.

Wheat, R. A. "The Federal Flextime System: Comparison and

Implementation." *Political Personnel Management*, 1982, *11* (1), 22–30.

Whetten, D. A., and Bozeman, B. "Policy Coordination and Interorganizational Relations." In J. Bryson and R. Einsweiler (eds.), *Sharing Power*. New York: University Press of America, forthcoming.

Whorton, J. W., and Worthley, J. A. "A Perspective on the Challenge of Public Management: Environmental Paradox and Organizational Culture." *Academy of Management Review*, 1981, *6*, 357–362.

Williamson, O. E. "The Economics of Organization: The Transaction Cost Approach." *American Journal of Sociology*, 1981a, *87* (3), 548–577.

Williamson, O. E. *Market and Hierarchies*. New York: Free Press, 1981b.

Wilson, J. Q. "The Rise of the Bureaucratic State." *Public Interest*, 1975, *41*, 77–103.

Wilson, J. Q., and Rachal, P. "Can Government Regulate Itself?" *Public Interest*, 1977, *46*, 3–14.

Wilson, W. "The Study of Administration." *Political Science Quarterly*, 1887, *2*, 197–222.

Wolf, C. "A Theory of Non-Market Failure." *Public Interest*, 1979, *55*, 114–133.

Woll, P. *American Bureaucracy*. (2nd ed.) New York: Norton, 1977.

Yarwood, D. L., and Enis, B. J. "Advertising and Publicity Programs in the Executive Branch of the National Government." *Public Administration Review*, 1982, *42* (1), 37–46.

Zif, J. "Managerial Strategic Behavior in State-Owned Enterprises: Business and Political Orientations." *Management Science*, 1981, *27*, 1326–1339.

Index

A

Abernathy, W., 148
Abramson, M. A., 17
Acme Aviation, as Public Generic type, 118
Adams, B., 19, 21
Advanced Population Laboratory, as Public Market type, 130
Advanced Turbine Research, as Quasi-Public Market type, 131, 132
Aerospace industry: goal processes in, 11-12; organization life cycles in, 9-10; political authority for, 7, 13; publicness of, 7-13; resource publicness in, 7-9; as special case, 13; and structural processes, 10-11
Air Commerce Act of 1926, 10
Air Mail Act of 1925, 10
Alchian, A. A., 52, 53-54, 56
Aldrich, H., 25, 92
Allison, G. T., Jr., 2, 41
American Bar Association, and political authority, 64, 77
American Telephone and Telegraph (AT&T): Bell Laboratories of, 107; and secondary political authority, 72
Anderson, W., 23
Appleby, P. H., 14, 41
Arendt, H., 66

Argonne National Laboratory, publicness of, 108
Atomic Energy Laboratory, as Public Multi-Market type, 123, 124
Australia, airlines in, 57
Authority: as base of organization, 5; concept of, 47; limits of, in personnel system, 17, 18; mediation of, 90; for policy making and for implementation, 21. See also Economic authority; Political authority
Authority mix: concept of, 85; and mediation, 90-91; publicness as, 84, 85, 93-94; and publicness grid, 94-96

B

Baas, L. R., 74
Backoff, R. W., 2, 33, 41
Baesel, J., 31
Bellante, D., 56
Benn, S. I., 32, 43, 145
Bennett, W. L., 63
Berle, A. A., 58
Beyer, J. M., 91
Black, E., 23
Black Forest Energy Lab, as Independent Market type, 133
Blau, P., 6, 25, 26
Bluestone, B., 10, 12
Blumberg, P. I., 77

175

Blumenthal, W. M., 2, 20, 41
Boundary spanning, as mediating
    act, 91-92
Bower, J., 52-53
Bozeman, B., 3, 7, 31, 40, 41, 42,
    47n, 91, 97, 100, 107n, 109, 111,
    113, 117, 138, 140, 143, 149
Breton, A., 34, 43, 47, 51
Broedling, L. A., 20
Brookhaven National Laboratory,
    publicness of, 108
Bruggink, T. H., 55
Buchanan, B., 3, 15-16, 17, 33, 42
Buchanan, J., 51

C

Califano, J., 2, 20
California Cyclotron Center, as
    Quasi-Public Generic type, 120
Cameron, K. S., 3
Campbell, A., 16
Capon, N., 56
Cathcart, P., 23
Caulfield, S. C., 21
Cayer, N. J., 17
Center for Advanced Energy Phys-
    ics, as Independent Generic
    type, 122
Chemical Processing Institute, as
    Independent Generic type, 121,
    122, 123
Cheung, S., 52
Child, J., 25
Chrysler Corporation, government
    loans to, 13
Civil Aeronautics Board, and or-
    ganizational life cycles, 100
Civil Service Reform Act of 1978,
    16
Clark, R. T., Jr., 31
Clarkson, K. W., 52, 53, 56-57, 58
Cleveland, R., 11
Cobb, R., 63
Cochran, C. E., 60
Committee for Economic Develop-
    ment, 30
Compliance, authority related to,
    47

Comsat, and tertiary political
    authority, 77
Constitution, and policy system
    elements, 74-75
Constraint: concepts of, 92; endow-
    ment equivalent with, 86-87;
    and publicness, 92-93
Copernicus, N., 143
Crandall, N., 24
Crow, M. M., 22, 42, 107n, 109, 113,
    117, 138, 140
Cummings, M. C., Jr., 18-19
Cunningham, W. G., 11

D

Dahl, R. A., 61, 143, 145, 146
Dalton, D. R., 24
Davies, D. G., 52, 53, 55, 56, 57
De Alessi, L., 52, 54, 58
Demac, D., 23
Demsetz, H., 52, 53-54
Desai, U., 22
Di Lorenzo, T. J., 54, 55
Dobratz, B. A., 69
Downs, A., 47, 51, 53, 91, 103-104
Dunsire, A., 25, 37, 42
Dupree, A. H., 107
Durant, R. F., 23
Dutton, W., 36

E

Eonomic authority: analysis of, 47-
    59; background on, 47; incre-
    ments of, 93; market failure
    model of, 49-50; minimalist
    model of, 48; political authority
    effects on, 81-82; property rights
    theory of, 49, 51-59; and public-
    ness, 48-50
Edelman, M., 60, 62
Eells, R., 77
Efficiency, concepts of, 35-36
Elder, C., 63
Emery, F. E., 91
Energy Engineering, as Quasi-
    Public Market type, 131, 132

Energy Pollution Research Laboratory, as Public Generic type, 118, 119
Energy Research, as Quasi-Public Generic type, 120, 121
Enis, B. J., 31
Environmental Protection Agency, and goal processes, 12
Equal Employment Opportunity (EEO): and secondary political authority, 73; and structural processes, 102
Etzioni, A., 6
Europe: hybrid organizations in, 31, 32; research institutes in, 129
Ewing Oil R & D, as Independent Multi-Market type, 128
Externalities, and public goods, 51

F

Federal Aviation Administration, and organizational life cycles, 10
Fiedler, F., 24
Finney, G., 30
Fitch, L. C., 36
Forrestal, J., 22
Fottler, M. D., 43
Fowlkes, F., 9
France, Super Phoenix Breeder Project in, 32
Frankel, C., 64
Fraser, J., 62
Frech, H. E., 58
Freeman, J. H., 39
Friedman, M., 48
Friedrich, C., 60, 62
Frost, P., 24
Fusfeld, H., 109

G

Galbraith, J., 48, 58
Gaus, G. F., 32, 43, 145
General Accounting Office (GAO): and secondary political authority, 73, 75; and structural processes, 102

General Energy, as Quasi-Public Multi-Market type, 125, 126
General Services Administration (GSA): and secondary political authority, 74, 75; and structural processes, 101
Gillo, M., 24
Goal processes: in aerospace industry, 11-12; and multi-dimensional theory, 103-105
Goals, reflexive and transitive, 103
Goodsell, C. T., 34, 82
Governance structure: concept of, 67, 73; and policy routines, 73, 75-76; and publicness of process, 73-74
Government: agencies of, and tertiary political authority, 77; legitimacy of, 69; and market failure model, 49-50; and minimalist model, 48; policies of, 70-71; and property rights theory, 49, 51-59; role and scope of, 69-70
Government-sponsored enterprises (GSEs), as hybrid, 31
Grace Commission, and efficiency, 35
Grady, R., 65
Grafstein, R., 63
Graham, F., 11
Graham, G. J., 43-44
Greenstein, F., 71
Grupp, F. W., 16
Gulick, L., 143
Gusfield, J. R., 34
Guyot, J. F., 17

H

Haas, J., 26
Hall, R., 6, 26
Hannigan, J. A., 64
Hayes, F. O., 2
Hayes, R., 148
Henry, N., 143
Herber, B., 50
Herbst, P. G., 24
Herker, D., 92

Heron, R. P., 42
Hess, R., 71
Heydebrand, V., 26
Hibbs, D. A., 70
Hickson, D. J., 24, 25, 42
Hinings, C. R., 24, 25
Hobbes, T., 63
Hoenack, S. A., 47
Holdaway, E., 42
Holmes, R., 66
Hood, C., 25, 37, 42
Hoover, H., 36
Hoover Commission, and efficiency, 35
Hopkins, R. H., 17
Horwitch, M., 32
Hulin, C. L., 29

I

Independent Generic laboratories, cases of, 114, 115, 121-123
Independent Market laboratories, cases of, 113, 114, 115, 132-134, 136, 139
Independent Multi-Market laboratories, cases of, 114, 115, 127-129, 136
Indiana Institute, as Independent Generic type, 121, 122, 123
Institute for Advanced Energy Research, as Public Generic type, 118
Institute for Solar System Development, as Quasi-Public Generic type, 120
Institute of Superconductivity, as Quasi-Public Multi-Market type, 125, 126
International Business Machines (IBM), Watson Research Center of, 107
Interstate Commerce Commission (ICC), and constraint, 92

J

James, D. R., 58
Jennings, M. K., 18-19

Jensen, M. C., 52
Johnson, N., 26
Jordan, P., 10, 12

K

Kahn, R., 6
Kann, M. E., 63-64
Katz, D., 6
Kaufman, H., 3, 26-27, 35, 38, 41, 70
Kelsen, H., 63, 66
Kilpatrick, F. P., 18-19
Kimberly, J., 24, 70
Kogod, R. P., 21
Kotler, P. E., 31
Kourvetaris, G., 69
Kraemer, K., 36
Kruybosch, C., 91
Kueneman, R. M., 64
Kuhn, T., 143, 144

L

Langlois, R., 109
Laser Science Center, as Public Generic type, 118, 119
Lau, A. W., 20
Lee, B., 12
Legitimacy: assessments of, 69; concepts of, 61-64; consent theory of, 62-63, 65; dialectical nature of, 63-64; legal positivist theory of, 63, 65, 67; and political authority, 61-66; and public organization theory, 64-66
Lerner, A. W., 38
Levenson, A. B., 23
Levine, C. H., 2, 33, 41, 70
Life cycles. *See* Organization life cycles
Lindblom, C. E., 47, 62, 145, 146
Lindsay, C. M., 55
Link, A. N., 56, 100, 138
Lipset, S., 66
Locke, J., 62
Lockheed, life cycle of, 9, 10
Loveless, S., 3, 42, 47n, 109, 111
Lovich, N. P., 17

Lowery, D., 19
Lowi, T. J., 61
Lynn, L. E., 2, 21, 22
Lynn, N., 17

M

McKelvey, B., 38
McNamara, R., 10, 35
McWilliams, W. C., 62
Madison, J., 64
Magnetic Science Center, as Quasi-Public Generic type, 120
Magnetic Transport Center, as Quasi-Public Multi-Market type, 125, 126
Mahoney, T., 24
Mainzer, L. C., 61
Management: "bottom line" and mixed motives types of, 147-149; education for, 152-153; and goal publicness, 104-105; and interdependence, 149-150; and life-cycle publicness, 100-101; and resource publicness, 98-99; and structural publicness, 102-103; and values, 150-152
Marcson, S., 109
Marini, F., 143
Marshall, W., 42
Martin, R., 63, 64
Martin Marietta Corporation, and publicness, 108
Masterman, M., 143
Mazzolini, R., 31
Means, G. C., 58
Meckling, W. H., 52
Mediating assumption, in multi-dimensional theory, 88-92
Medicare-Medicaid, 13
Merelman, R. M., 60, 64
Metalville Research Center, as Independent Market type, 133
Methe, D., 31
Mexico, assessments of legitimacy of state in, 69
Meyer, J. W., 1
Meyer, M. W., 25-26, 42
Miles, R. H., 70, 91

Mineral Research Laboratories, as Independent Multi-Market type, 128
Mintzberg, H., 149, 151
Mitnick, B., 34
Moe, T., 59
Mohr, L. B., 29, 103
Moore, L. F., 38
Morgan, R. J., 64
Mosher, F. C., 41
Mowery, D., 107
Multi-dimensional theory: analysis of, 83-106; application of, 105-106; assumptions in, 83, 84-86, 88-92; and authority mix, 93-94; axioms in, 84-87; background on, 83-84; constraint and publicness in, 92-93; and decomposition, 86; dynamics of, 87-96; and equivalency, 86-87; and goal processes, 103-105; mediating assumption in, 88-92; and organizational life cycle, 99-101; and organizational processes, 96-101; quantity and proportion in, 94-96; and resource processes, 96-99; and structural processes, 101-103
Multi-organization enterprises (MOEs): as hybrid, 31-32; and tertiary political authority, 77
Musolf, L., 5, 77

N

National Comparative R & D Laboratory Project (NCRL): case studies from, 116-134; and diversity, 109-116; findings from, 134-141
National Science Board, legitimacy of, 64
National Science Foundation, and cooperative research centers, 139
Neghandhi, A. R., 24
Nelson, O. T., 18
Neuberg, L. G., 55
Neutron Institute, as Public Generic type, 118

Newbery, J. F., 42
Newman, A. R., 20
Newton, I., 143
Nicaragua, assessment of policies toward, 71
Niskanen, W. A., 53
Nystrom, P. C., 1, 3, 27-28

O

Oak Ridge National Laboratory, publicness of, 108
Occupational Safety and Health Administration (OSHA): and secondary political authority, 72; and structural processes, 102
Office of Management and Budget (OMB): and secondary political authority, 74, 75; and structural processes, 101, 102
Office of Personnel Management (OPM): research by, 17; and secondary political authority, 74; and structural processes, 102
Olsen, J. B., 36
O'Neill, T. P., 70
Organization life cycles: in aerospace industry, 9-10; and multidimensional theory, 99-101; and primary political authority, 70; research on, 26-28
Organizations: authority base of, 5; barriers to knowledge on publicness of, 29-46; behavior affected by publicness of, 1-13; blurring of sectors of, 30-32; boundary spanning by, 91-92; and causal problem, 40; concept of, 6; essential processes of, 7, 96; hybrid, 31-32; measurement and construct validity issues of, 37-39; mediation of authority in, 90; multi-dimensional theory and, 89; and organizers and organizing, 40; and political authority, 68-78; and primary political authority, 68-71; processes of, and publicness, 96-101; publicness dimensions of, 5,

83-106; research and development, case examples of, 107-141; resource buffers in, 91; and secondary political authority, 72-76; technology buffers in, 91; and tertiary political authority, 76-78; triadic model of effects of political authority on, 79-80. See also Private organizations; Public organizations
Ostrom, V., 143
Ownership. See Property rights

P

Padgett, L., 69
Palmer, J., 2, 70
Pearce, J. L., 16
Peltzman, S., 52
Pendleton Act of 1889, 17
Perry, J. L., 3, 16
Personnel: attitudes of, 15-17; motivation of, 3; research on, 15-19; self-selection of, 18-19; structure and procedures of systems for, 17-18
Pfeffer, J., 100, 149
Photo Chemicals, as Independent Multi-Market type, 127, 128
Pinder, C. C., 38
Policy routines, and governance structures, 73, 75-76
Policy system elements: and Constitution, 74-75; and governance structures, 73
Political authority: for aerospace industry, 7, 13; analysis of, 60-82; background on, 60-61; buffers of, 88-92; complexity of effects of, 78-79; constraint and endowment equivalent in, 86-87; economic authority affected by, 81-82; endowment types of, 66-68; and essential processes, 7; increments of, 94; and legitimacy, 61-66; and organizations, 68-78; primary, 66, 68-71; and resource mix, 97; secondary, 66-67, 72-76, 93; tertiary, 67-68, 76-

78; triadic model of, 78–82; value dimension of, 151–152
Ponzer, B. Z., 3
Pool, I., 82
Porter, L. W., 3
Power Systems Laboratory, as Independent Market type, 132, 133
Prahalad, C., 32
Primary political authority: concept of, 66; levels of influence in, 68–71
Private organizations: compared with public, 14–28; and economic authority, 84, 85; as minigovernments, 77–78; personnel and personnel systems in, 15–19; political authority vested in, 67–68, 77; publicness of, 7–13; structures of, 23–28; work contexts of, 19–23
Privateness: and economic authority, 47–59; and property rights theory, 51–59; and public goods, 50–51, 57; theory of, 59
Property rights: as economic authority theory, 49, 51–59; empirical tests of, 55–57; evaluation of, 57–59; and monitoring, 54–55; and oversight, 53–54; and reward and incentives, 52–53
Provan, K., 91
Provincial Mining Laboratory, as Public Market type, 129, 130
Public Generic laboratories, cases of, 113, 114, 115, 116, 117–119, 129, 134, 136, 138–139
Public goods: concepts of, 50; and privateness, 50–51, 57
Public Market laboratories, cases of, 114, 115, 129, 130, 132
Public Multi-Market laboratories, cases of, 114, 115, 123–125
Public organizations: aggregation issues for, 39; as authority mix, 84, 85, 93–94; barriers to understanding, 29–40; basis of theory of, 61, 83; case studies of, 41, 44; coding issues for, 37–38; comparative sector research on, 42,

44; compared with private, 14–28; conceptualizing, 32–37; as economic character, 33–34; generic research on, 42–43, 44, 45; as government, 33; incidental, 42–43, 44, 45; and legitimacy, 64–66; level of analysis of, 38–39; personnel and personnel systems in, 15–19; and political authority, 84–85; practitioner accounts of, 41, 44; as public interest, 34–35; single-sector research on, 42, 44–45; structures of, 23–28; theoretical frameworks for, 43, 44; work contexts of, 19–23
Publicness: aggregate and binary approaches to, 44–46; analysis of puzzle of, 1–13; analytic problem of, 32–37; approaches to, 41–43; assumptions about, 4–5; as authority mix, 93–94; background on, 1–2; barriers to knowledge on, 29–46; case examples of, 107–141; causal problem of, 40; classifying, 110–113; concept of, 61; conceptualizing, 4–5; and constraint, 92–93; and constraint and endowment equivalency, 86–87; dimensions of, 5, 83–106; disaggregated, 86; economic and political authority mixed in, 82; and economic authority, 48–50; generalization-seeking approaches to, 44–46; and goal processes, 11–12, 103–105; and governance structures, 73–74; grid of, 94–96; ideographic approaches to, 43–44; implications of, 142–154; influence of, 6–7; and interdependence, 149–150; issues involving, 3–4; and legal status, 85; and management education, 152–153; and managerial values, 150–152; managing, 147–149; measure of, 111; methodological problem of, 37–39; multi-dimensional view of, 83–106; normative and ideological confusion about, 35–37; and or-

ganization life cycles, 9-10; and organization processes, 96-101; as paradigm, 142-144; political authority at root of, 60-82; of private organizations, 7-13; and property rights theory, 51-59; and public management, 146-152; as research and theory paradigm, 144-146; of resource processes, 7-9, 96-99; stakes in, 2-4; and structural processes, 10-11, 101-103; synthetic problem of, 30-32; as taproot for research, education, and practice, 154; and triadic model of political authority, 80-82; typology of approaches to, 43-46; typology of, for R & D organizations, 113-116

Pugh, D. S., 24, 25

Q

Quasi-Public Generic laboratories, cases of, 114, 115, 119-121
Quasi-Public Market laboratories, cases of, 114, 115, 129, 131-132, 136
Quasi-Public Multi-Market laboratories, cases of, 114, 115, 125-126, 134, 136

R

Rachel, P., 23
Rainey, H. G., 2, 3, 16, 17, 19, 33, 41, 42
Ravetz, J., 143
Rawls, J. R., 18, 63
Reagan, R., 20, 35, 36
Reagan administration: and assessment of role and scope of state, 69-70; civil service responses to, 19; and privatization, 138; and technology transfer, 2
Redford, E., 34
Regional Energy Research Center, as Quasi-Public Market type, 131, 132

Reimann, B. C., 24
Research: background on, 14-15; case studies in, 41, 44; comparative sector type of, 42, 44; comparing public and private organizations, 14-28; generic type of, 42-43, 44, 45; incidental type of, 42-43, 44, 45; on personnel and personnel systems, 15-19; practitioner accounts in, 41, 44; single-sector type of, 42, 44-45; on structures, 23-28; theoretical frameworks in, 43, 44; Type A and Type B errors in, 46, 153; on work contexts, 19-23
Research and development (R & D) organizations: analysis of performance of, 107-141; background on, 107-109; case studies of, 116-134; classifying population of, 109-110; classifying publicness of, 110-113; cooperative, 139; direct support of, 138; diversity of, 109-116; effectiveness implications of, 140-141; findings on, 134-141; findings on, 134-141; hypotheses about, 137; privateness measure of, 112-113; privatization of, 138-139; public policy implications of, 137-140; publicness measure for, 111; publicness typology for, 113-116; and research planning, 136; research scope of, 134; stability of, 136; structure of, 136-137; and tax credits, 139-140; and technical change, 134-136; theoretical implications of, 141
Resources: in aerospace industry, 7-9; as buffers, 91; and multidimensional theory, 96-99
Retired Executive Corps, and organizational life cycles, 101
Revans, R. W., 24
Rhinehart, J. B., 3, 42
Rice, B., 9
Richard, A. R., 16
Ring, P. S., 16
Roberts, K. H., 29

Robinson, R., 54, 55
Roessner, J. D., 2
Roosevelt, F. D., 69
Rose, R., 36
Rosen, B., 17
Rothschild, J., 60
Rousseau, D. M., 29
Rowan, B., 1, 42
Roy, W. G., 67
Rumsfeld, D., 2, 41
Runciman, W. G., 61
Rusbult, C. E., 19
Rushing, W., 42

S

Salancik, G., 149
Samuelson, P., 49
Savas, E. S., 4
Sawhill, I., 2, 70
Schaar, J. H., 61
Schiesl, M. H., 36
Schmidt, R. E., 17
Schmidt, W. W., 3
Schoenherr, R., 25
Schulman, S., 31
Scott, W. R., 6
Seattle Tech, as Independent Multi-Market type, 128
Secondary political authority: concept of, 66-67; and constraint, 93; and governance structures, 73-74; and organizations, 72-76; and policy routines, 75-76; and policy system elements, 74-75
Segal, M., 3
Seidman, H., 5
Selznick, P., 41
Service allocation, and publicness, 4
Shaffer, P. L., 17
Sharkansky, I., 75-76
Shaw, L. C., 31
Shelton, J., 53
Shirking, and property rights theory, 53-54
Shubert, G., 34
Sidney, J. L., 31
Simon, H., 143

Simonson, G. R., 10, 12
Small Business Administration, and organizational life cycles, 101
Smart, C., 22
Smith, S. P., 31
Smith Chemical Research Laboratory, as Independent Market type, 132, 133
Soref, M., 58
Southwest Mining Laboratory, as Public Market type, 129, 130
Starbuck, W. H., 1, 3, 27-28
State Energy Lab, as Public Multi-Market type, 123, 124
Stauffer, R., 26
Steckler, H., 7
Stillman, P., 63, 66
Straussman, J. D., 31, 97, 149
Structures: life spans of, 26-28; processes of, 10-11, 101-103; research on, 23-28; of R & D organizations, 136-137; size of, 24
Sullivan, M., 10, 12

T

Taft, R. A., 70
Taylor, F., 143
Technology: as buffers, 91; transfer of, and publicness, 2-3
Tennessee Valley Authority, and tertiary political authority, 77
Tertiary political authority: concept of, 67-68; and organizations, 76-78
Thompson, J., 91, 98
Tolbert, P. S., 42, 76
Trist, E. L., 91
Turner, C., 24
Tussman, J., 63

U

Ullrich, R. A., 18
Underwater Energy Systems Center, as Public Market type, 130
United Kingdom, organizational structures in, 25, 37

U.S. Civil Service System, compared with private organizations, 16, 17–18

U.S. Department of Defense (DOD): and efficiency, 35; Independent Research and Development (IRAD) organizations of, 108; and political authority, 71, 73, 75; and structural processes, 10–11

U.S. Department of Energy: national laboratories of, 108, 138; and tertiary political authority, 77

Urwick, L., 143

V

Vaden, R. E., 17
Validity, issues of, 37–39
Values, managerial, 150–152
Vertinsky, I., 22
Vietnam, and primary political authority, 66
Vinson-Trammell Act, 9
Vogel, D., 34, 77–78

W

Walsh, A. H., 31
Wamsley, G. L., 3, 43, 145, 146

Warwick, D. P., 1, 41
Weber, M., 6, 25, 60, 145
Weick, K., 40
Weissberg, R., 71
Weitzel, W., 24
Wheat, R. A., 31
Whetten, D. A., 3, 91, 149
Whorton, J. W., 3
Williams, R. O., 42
Williamson, O. E., 34, 51
Wilson, J. Q., 23, 75
Wilson, W., 41
Winetrobe, R., 34, 43, 47, 51
Wolf, C., 50
Woll, P., 74, 92
Work contexts; research on, 19–23; stakes in, 23, time frame and pace of, 19–22; visibility of, 22–23
Worthley, J. A., 3

Y

Yale, D. A., 17
Yarwood, D. L., 31

Z

Zald, M. N., 3, 43, 145, 146
Zucker, L. G., 42, 76